COMBATING PIRACY

Intellectual Property Theft and Fraud

COMBATING PIRACY

Edited by
JAY S. ALBANESE

Transaction Publishers
New Brunswick (U.S.A.) and London (U.K.)

First paperback edition 2009
Copyright © 2007 by Transaction Publishers, New Brunswick, New Jersey.

All rights reserved under International and Pan-American Copyright Conventions. No part of this book may be reproduced or transmitted in any form or by any means, electronic or mechanical, including photocopy, recording, or any information storage and retrieval system, without prior permission in writing from the publisher. All inquiries should be addressed to Transaction Publishers, Rutgers—The State University, 35 Berrue Circle, Piscataway, New Jersey 08854-8042. www.transactionpub.com

This book is printed on acid-free paper that meets the American National Standard for Permanence of Paper for Printed Library Materials.

Library of Congress Catalog Number: 2006045604
ISBN: 978-0-7658-0357-3 (cloth); 978-1-4128-1146-0 (paper)
Printed in the United States of America

Library of Congress Cataloging-in-Publication Data

Combating piracy : intellectual property theft and fraud / Jay S. Albanese, editor.
    p. cm.
Includes bibliographical references and index.
Contents: Fraud: the characteristic crime of the twenty-first century / Jay S. Albanese—Intellectual property theft and organized crime: the case of film piracy / Jeffrey Scott McIllwain—Causes and prevention of intellectual property crime / Nicole Leeper Piquero—Intellectual property and white-collar crime: report of issues, trends, and problems for future research / Annette Beresford ... [et al.]—Addressing the global scope of intellectual property crimes and policy initiatives / Hedieh Nasheri—Report of the Task Force on Intellectual Property / U.S. Department of Justice.
    ISBN 0-7658-0357-7 (alk. paper)
    1. Fraud. 2. Intellectual property infringement. 3. Intellectual property infringement—Prevention. I. Albanese, Jay S.

HV6691.C662   2006
364.16'3—dc22   2006045604

Contents

Introduction

Jay S. Albanese

Manifestations of fraud in the early twenty-first century are showing signs of innovation and adaptation in response to shifting opportunities. This book reports on new analyses of intellectual property theft as its most recent expression. Fraud and piracy of products and ideas have become common as the opportunities to commit them expand, and technology exists that make them easy to carry out. Consider some examples:

- A nineteen-year-old movie theatre employee in St. Louis pled guilty to using a camcorder to copy new releases and upload them to a computer network in California for illegal distribution. He admitted to linking a camcorder to the theater sound board, later synchronizing the audio with the video using his personal computer. According to the Motion Picture Association of America, more than 90 percent of piracy of new movie releases involves the use of camcorders inside movie theaters (First, 2005).
- A twenty-seven-year-old Ukrainian pled guilty to selling counterfeit computer software using several different web sites, disguising his identity, and using intermediaries in the United States to forward him funds to an account in Lithuania (Guilty, 2005).
- A sixty-two-year-old woman in Pennsylvania pled guilty as a participant in "Warez" underground community that used the Internet to engage in large-scale, illegal distribution of copyrighted software, video games, movies, and music files. The plea was part of "Operation Safehaven," which was the largest seizure to date of a Warez site, pirated CDs, DVDs and computers by the U.S. government (Operation Safehaven, 2005).

These cases illustrate the wide-ranging nature of the activity, and the spectrum of persons involved in piracy of intellectual property. Intellectual property theft is comprised of copyrights, trademarks, trade secrets, and patents, which represent the creative work of individuals for which others cannot claim credit. Copyrights protect written work, such as books, music, movies, art, and plays, trademarks protect brand names and images, trade secrets (such as the recipe for Coke) protect developers of unique ideas or formulas, and patents protect new inventions. The protection of intellectual property exists to properly credit and compensate those whose ideas and products are distributed by others. The distributors of books, movies, music, and other forms of intellectual property pay for this right, and those who distribute this work without compensation to its creator effectively hijack or "pirate" that property without the owner's or distributor's permission (and without compensation).

Concern about intellectual property theft rises above the level of unscrupulous individuals. There is growing frustration with countries, such as China and Russia, which have had a poor record of enforcement intellectual property rights by allowing widespread counterfeiting of American brand name products (Forney, 2005; Riskind, 2005; U.S. Government Accountability Office, 2004). In one case a U.S. citizen ran an Internet site from Shanghai, China, called ThreeDollarDVD. com. The web site was hosted in Russia, and he sold thousands of pirated copies of movies that he bought through eBay from Chinese manufacturers for 50 cents each. The indictment alleged that he made more than $1 million before being caught by purchasers who were undercover agents. In another case a fifty-two-year-old man from Washington State was arrested along with eleven Chinese nationals for distributing counterfeit pharmaceuticals, including Viagra, Cialis, and Lipitor (Waterman, 2005).

The problem has grown to the point where most software in China, Russia, Thailand, India, Brazil, and the Middle East is pirated (Fordahl, 2005). The World Health Organization estimates that 10 percent of all pharmaceuticals available worldwide are counterfeit (Israel, 2005). Such widespread fraud illustrates the global reach of the problem and the need for international remedies that include changed attitudes, public education, increasing the likelihood of apprehension, and reducing available opportunities.

The chapters in this book examine the problem of piracy of intellectual property from different perspectives. It is a form of fraud, a form of organized crime, a white-collar crime, a criminal activity with causes we can isolate and prevent, and it is a global problem. The readings in this book examine each of these perspectives to determine how they can contribute to our understanding of the issues involved. Four of the contributions were carried out with the support of the National Institute of Justice and the efforts of its International Center to develop a better understanding of the state of knowledge and the important research questions to be addressed in the coming years.

The opening chapter in this book places fraud in context as part of a larger shift away from mere larceny toward larceny by trick. Larceny remains the most common of all serious crimes, but fraud is overtaking larceny, because of changes in our ownership, storage, and movement of property. Entrusting property to the custody of others, storing property at remote locations, and electronic movement of property reflect major changes in the way we treat property and increase opportunities for theft. The motivation of theft behind many frauds is also shown to be used to fund larger criminal objectives, such as illegal immigration and terrorism.

Jeffrey Scott McIllwain documents through media, government, and industry sources, the problems in obtaining a full understanding the connection of organized crime to film piracy. Nevertheless, recent efforts to strengthen laws and enforcement have paid considerable dividends for the intellectual property industries as a whole. In the U.S. and across the globe, seizures, criminal indictments, civil actions, and public awareness are up considerably. Whether or not these advances can be maintained in the face of technological advances, the evolution of industry economic structures, consumer indifference to the stigma of intellectual property theft, and anger at industry responses to such theft, remains to be seen.

Nicole Leeper Piquero examines the four categories of intellectual property (patents, trademarks, trade secrets, and copyright) and the attention they have attracted because of illicit copying of software, movies, videogames, and music that deny publishers and authors' economic returns on their property. She identifies the types of activities that fall under the rubric of intellectual property, and develops the causes and theoretical arguments to understand the existence and growth of intellectual property theft. The chapter also assesses alternate prevention techniques to control and prevent the misuse and theft of intellectual property.

Annette Beresford, Christian Desilets, Sandy Haantz, John Kane, and April Wall examine the association between intellectual property theft and other white-collar crimes, including investment fraud, money laundering, identity theft, and other offenses. The authors review data on intellectual property violations related to white collar crime, and focus on impacts and strategies related to intellectual property laws and enforcement practices. They find a need for more adequate support, coordination, and education among the general public and within the law enforcement and business communities.

Hedieh Nasheri traces the current need for an international effort to protect intellectual property to the Industrial Revolution when new manufacturing techniques and new industrial products were developed and exported, increasing commercial and cultural relations between countries. She identifies the need to build international public awareness of the role of intellectual property in fostering a broad understanding and respect for the system that promotes and protects intellectual property rights. This chapter provides a survey of the current worldwide response to intellectual property crime and raises policy considerations for the future.

The Task Force on Intellectual Property offers a look at the government's best thinking on this issue, summarizing what it has done and, more importantly, what needs to be done in the areas of enforcement and prevention both in the U.S. and internationally. Reporting in late 2004, the recommendations of this Department of Justice report offer a useful comparison to the analyses of the other authors of this volume, and it will be interesting to see the extent to which they are implemented in the coming years, and their ultimate impact on intellectual property crimes.

This book offers an early synthesis of the dimensions of intellectual property theft and fraud and its relation to and impact on criminal justice research and practice. Combating piracy of intellectual property is a crucial concern because it lies at the heart of innovation—the world of creative ideas, research, and invention are at the root of a dynamic economy, new products, and a vital citizenry. As Irving Louis Horowitz has suggested, a global approach is needed: "If social science is to earn the right to be called a science, then its findings must be validated in global, not just national terms" (2000). This has never been more true than it is in combating intellectual property theft and fraud, where creative expression and new ideas will form the basis for the quality of life in the years to come. It is hoped that this analysis will spur the next wave of inspired thinking and empirical research in this new area of criminological concern.

References

First Conviction Made under New Copyright Law. (2005). *Washington Internet Daily.* Vol. 6, no. 188. September 28.

Fordahl, Matthew. (2005). U.S. to Send Teams to Combat Piracy Abroad. *Associated Press Financial Wire.* September 21.

Forney, Matthew. (2005). Faking It: Beijing's Inability to Curb Rampant Intellectual Property Theft is Infuriating Its Trading Partners. *Time International.* vol. 165. June 13.

Guilty Plea in International Software Piracy and Financial Crime Prosecution. (2005). *States News Service.* November 29.

Horowitz, Irving Louis. (2000). Globalizing Social Science. *Society.* Vol. 37, Issue 3. March. p. 83.

Israel, Chris. (2005). Chinese and Russian Enforcement of Intellectual Property Rights. Testimony before U.S. House Judiciary Committee Subcommittee on Courts, the Internet, and Intellectual Property. *Federal Document Clearinghouse Congressional Testimony.* December 7.

Operation Safehaven: Pennsylvania Woman Pleads Guilty to Federal Software Piracy Charge. (2005). *States News Service.* September 27.

Riskind, Jonathan. (2005). Business Owner Testifies about Intellectual Property Theft. *The Columbus Dispatch.* June 15.

U.S. Government Accountability Office. (2004). *Intellectual Property: U.S. Efforts Have Contributed to Strengthened Laws Overseas, but Challenges Remain.* Washington, DC: September 8.

Waterman, Shawn. (2005). Man Arraigned on China DVD Piracy Charges. *United Press International.* October 26.

1

Fraud: The Characteristic Crime of the Twenty-first Century

Jay S. Albanese
Virginia Commonwealth University

In the same way that larceny characterized much of twentieth century, fraud will likely characterize the twenty-first century. Larceny, defined as taking property of another with intent to deprive the owner, remained at high levels throughout the 1900s, and is the most common of all crimes. In the United States, for example, larcenies reported to police rose from 4.3 million during the 1970s to 7.1 million by 2002 (Federal Bureau of Investigation, 2004). Victimization surveys (including both crimes reported to police as well as those unreported) revealed stable, but much higher levels of larcenies at approximately 14 million incidents per year, far surpassing the volume and rate per 1,000 population of any other serious crime (Bastian, Perkins, Rennison, and Ringel, 2004).

Fraud is defined as purposely obtaining the property of another through deception, and its popularity as a crime of choice is growing. The connection between fraud and many of the serious crimes of the twenty-first century can be seen from the facts of recent cases.

A two-year investigation into the illegal practices of Indonesian immigration brokers resulted in an indictment alleging that the owners, employees, and associates of these brokerages knowingly defrauded the government for several years. Thousands of Indonesian immigrants living throughout the United States were aided in fraudulently applying for a wide variety of government benefits through alien labor certification, Virginia driver's licenses and identification cards, United States passports, and Social Security cards. The investigation revealed that fraudulent asylum applications for Indonesian clients were prepared in return for a fee of $2,000 or more. These applications typically contained false claims that the applicant had been raped, sexually assaulted, beaten, or robbed by Muslims in Indonesia on account of the applicant's Chinese ethnicity or adherence to Christianity. The defendants often supported these claims with counterfeit Indonesian documents, such as birth certificates, baptismal certificates, and police reports. The investigation also revealed that these same defendants coached their clients to exploit the perceived sympathies of the asylum officers and immigration judges assigned to consider the applications. In addition, Indonesian clients were routinely aided to obtain Virginia Department of Motor Vehicles (DMV) driver's licenses, learner's permits and identification cards by fraud (U.S. Fed News, 2004).

The U.S. government brought fraud accusations against two Moroccan defendants originally charged in the first major terrorism trial since the September 11, 2001 attacks. The superseding indictment alleged that they devised a scheme to defraud Titan Insurance Company by filing false claims. The pair claimed they were injured in a July 5, 2001 auto accident and submitted fraudulent claims for lost wages, physical therapy, and household services. An alleged Detroit terror cell—which the government said included the four men—came to light six days after the World Trade Center attack when federal agents raided an apartment and found false IDs and other materials that the government claimed were blueprints for terror attacks (Associated Press, 2004).

These cases connect the simple motivation of theft that motivates many frauds with larger attempts at illegal immigration, false identity documents, terrorism, and other crimes, illustrating that fraud is often used to fund other criminal objectives. Why is fraud becoming a crime of choice among both thieves and those with larger criminal objectives?

Ownership and Storage

There has been a fundamental shift in the method by which property is owned. This shift has occurred for reasons of changes in technology, communications, and globalization. For much of the twentieth century, personal and business cash and property was kept physically on the premises, in safety deposit boxes, or in local banks. In every case, the owner had quick, direct physical access to the property at all times. This situation has changed. In contemporary society credit and debit transactions are overtaking cash transactions in volume, and personal property is increasingly leased or borrowed rather than owned. Therefore, fewer people are holding cash or valuables on their person or in their homes, making larceny less attractive as a crime.

Efforts to conceal ownership sometimes occur to either perpetrate a fraud or to conceal other kinds of criminal activity. A former employee of a used automobile dealership pleaded guilty to taking part in a complex money-laundering scheme intended to exchange drug sale proceeds for luxury vehicles. Invoices, financing and other documents were forged or altered to disguise customer identities and the true nature of financial transactions. The dealership was suspected of selling vehicles to known narcotics dealers and filing false forms in order to disguise the true purchaser of the vehicles (Jardini, 2004). This case illustrates how fraud can be used to disguise not only the source of funds needed to purchase property, but also conceal the actual owner of the property. Similar kinds of frauds have been used to conceal the identities of victims of trafficking in human beings, the smuggling of natural resources, and other kinds of theft, concealment, and illegal transport (United Nations Interregional Crime and Justice Research Institute, 2004; Warchol 2004; Krebs, 2004).

Movement

The movement of property has been made easier by the rise and growth of the Internet, facilitating wireless transactions and making the conversion of cash to property and property to cash easier. A director of The Gillette Company testified before the U.S. Congress that 34 million counterfeit Duracell batteries were seized in 2004, along with 31 million fake Gillette shaving products and tens of thousands of fake Oral-B toothbrushes. He estimated a $200 billion loss to the U.S. economy and a loss of 750,000 American jobs, asking Congress to pursue international avenues to promote enactment of mandatory confiscation and destruction laws, strengthened criminal penalties, and enhanced global cooperation on the issue. Fox further testified that "The majority of goods are stolen not for personal use but by organized criminals intent on the resale of the goods or to use them as collateral for other consumables such as drugs." This is carried out through organized retail theft rings, which "recruit gangs of shoplifters, giving them lists of low-volume, high-value items to be stolen from retail outlets items such as razor blades, batteries, over-the-counter drugs, infant formula, and designer clothing." Those caught are treated as individual shoplifters and are handled leniently, overlooking the organized crime connection behind the crimes (Fox, 2005). This suggests a larger profit motive behind these frauds than personal gain; instead, fraud becomes a self-supporting business with profit potential far beyond that of mere larceny. The scope of harm produced by larceny is usually limited to the value of the physical property taken, whereas fraud often involves re-selling of nonphysical property that has limitless value. For example one Internet posting on a known hacker website read, "I work in the fraud dept. for a well known U.S. company, and have access to hundreds of CCs (credit card numbers) on a daily basis. All I'm looking for is an easy way to make some money and stay anonymous..." He received the first of six inquiries within an hour, describing how to sell and use stolen private information quickly and easily sold over the Internet (Kirby, 2005).

Table 1.1 illustrates that arrests for fraud have increased substantially over the last thirty years. Whether changes in fraud are measured by arrests (up 171 percent) or by the rate of arrests per 100,000 population (+102 percent), which accounts for population growth, table 1.1 shows a substantial increase over time. But has fraud always been popular?

Protecting Property from Larceny

Perhaps the oldest form of criminal behavior is theft, and it remains the most common crime in all societies of all types. The most common form of theft, historically, has been larceny by stealth—

Table 1.1
Trends in Arrests for Fraud

Year	Number arrested	Rate per 100,000 population
1970	76,861	50.7
1980	261,787	125.7
1995	320,046	162.9
2003	208,469	102.2
Totals	+171 %	+102 %

that is, stealing by secretive or furtive means. Property owners over the years have taken great precautions to protect their property. Public police forces did not exist in most countries (including the United States) until the nineteenth century. Prior to that, citizens were responsible for protecting their own property, and they either armed themselves, hired bodyguards, or fashioned "safes" as places to store their valuables. Later in that century, banks became central repositories for valuable private property, when government currency and jewels came to be the primary indicators of wealth and the means for exchange.

The evolution of bank safes offers an interesting example of how theft has changed over time. As is still true today, patterns of theft from banks were strongly related to the available opportunities to steal. During the early twentieth century, safes were locked with a key. Thieves learned how to pick the locks, so the combination lock was invented. Criminals founds a way to pry the entire combination spindle from the safe, so sturdier locks were manufactured.

In an apparent response to this move, safecrackers drilled holes in the safes and inserted explosives to open them. Metals were then alloyed to make safe difficult to violate. Some criminals obtained nitroglycerin, which could be inserted into tiny crevices, or used oxy-acetylene torches to open safes. Safes soon appeared with perfectly fitted doors that could not be pried, drilled, melted, or penetrated by explosives.

Some criminals turned to kidnapping bankers, forcing them to open the safes, and the time lock was invented to prevent this. In a similar way, some burglars began to cart away the entire safe to be opened later, and safes were made larger and too heavy to move. Night depositories were also invented to provide businesspersons an alternative to keeping cash in their smaller store safes. Safes were later invented that would release gas when disturbed, so criminals equipped themselves with gas masks (Cressey, 1972).

This progression in the organization of thefts from bank safes illustrates an important factor in the history of theft. There is a relationship between the technology of crime and the technology of prevention. If changes in the nature of safecracking can be generalized to other forms of theft, it may be true that the more sophisticated the prevention technology (e.g., harder metals, time locks, etc.), the more sophisticated criminals must become to maintain acceptable levels of success (e.g., using explosives, kidnapping bankers, etc.).

Credit card fraud has endured a similar progression in frauds and fraud prevention. In the beginning banks that issued credit cards published regular listings of invalid numbers in booklet form, so merchants could see if a submitted card had been stolen or cancelled. The response of criminals was to steal a card and use it as any times as possible immediately thereafter to reach the credit limit before the stolen card number was published. Banks responded with magnetic tape readers in stores that communicated electronically with the bank's computer at the point of sale to determine the card's status, eliminating the need for published lists. Some thieves then took an alternate approach and went through store trash bins to retrieve used carbon forms credit-card purchases, which contain an imprint of the owner's account number and signature. This information could then be use to manufacture a duplicate card that would turn up as "valid," when used. More recently, carbonless receipts were developed, and three-dimensional holograms were added to credit cards to make them more difficult to duplicate. The dramatic growth of shopping online via the Internet created the need for the numeric code on the back of credit cards to insure that the online buyer actually had possession of the card being used.

"Dumpster diving used to be the number-one concern," ten years ago, according to director of fraud prevention and data security for American Express. Fraud prevention in that era consisted of tearing up carbon copies of sales slips. "These were very manual ways for people to collect information and perpetrate fraud," she says. "Now it's identity theft, 'phishing,' skimming" (Gardham, 2005). In skimming, thieves use a merchant's credit card reader to capture magnetic-stripe data and then re-encode credit and debit cards. The cards are then given to runners, who shop at malls, high-end jewelry stores, electronics stores, and other retailers. Phishing involves sending individuals an email request for information that appears to come from a legitimate company, store, or bank which asks recipients to verify confidential personal information, such as account numbers, social security numbers, passwords, or other sensitive information. This information is then used to unlawfully use that person's credit or bank account. As was shown above in the case of bank safes, the history of credit card fraud has shown the back-and-forth between the technology of criminals and the technology of law enforcement to keep pace.

Table 1.2 illustrates the changing nature of theft, depicting how changes in the way we own, store, and move property has changed in the electronic age. Access to cash and merchandise is now done remotely with ease, making possible identity theft, intellectual property theft, skimming and phishing, which have become modern forms of theft (now fraud), because information that provides access to cash or property (e.g., credit card, bank account information) involves less risk and more potential gain than attempts to steal the property directly through burglary or larceny.

Crime Prevention Technology Reacts to Criminal Technology

British sociologist Mary McIntosh has suggested that improvement in crime detection forces criminals to become more organized in order to remain successful. As she explains, "criminals and their opponents are thus engaged in an all-out war which has a tendency to escalate as each side improves its techniques to outwit the other" (McIntosh, 1975:52). Thieves plan and organize their behavior in order to minimize the risk of a direct confrontation with the victim, which might lead to violence—something almost always found undesirable by offenders. As a result, the primary goal of most thieves

Table 1.2
The Changing Nature of Theft

Older Manifestations of Theft	Modern Manifestations of Theft
Larceny and burglary (because property usually held on site)	Identity Theft (usually to gain access to the credit line/purchasing power of the owner)
Real property theft (cash, physical property)	Intellectual property theft (patents, trademarks, trade secrets, and copyright)
Pickpocketing and purse snatching (because property and cash often carried by individuals)	Skimming (theft of credit card information by deception, usually via electronic means) or Phishing (false e-mail solicitations to lure a suspect to divulge personal or credit information)
Risk higher (always the possibility of a face-to-face confrontation with the victim and the need to escape quickly from the crime scene to avoid apprehension)	Risk lower (never involves face-to-face contact with the victim, and no need for speed or agility because success

is sufficient organization to reduce the possibility of apprehension and, thereby, increase the chances for success.

Rapid changes in the global economy and technology, including worldwide access to the Internet, ease of communications with e-mail and mobile phones, and the rise of electronic buying, selling, and banking without the need for face-to-face transactions, have combined to create new opportunities that can be exploited by motivated offenders. Once thieves experience some success, the government and private industry take steps to reduce the opportunities for theft. This improvement in the detection and/or prevention technology is subsequently matched, and often surpassed, by criminals if they are to avoid apprehension.

Law, law enforcement, and prevention technology usually lag behind the innovative techniques of offenders in exploiting new criminal opportunities. Consider that street lighting is usually improved *after* a number of robberies occur on a dark street. The same can be said for steering-column locks on automobiles, burglar alarms in stores, cameras in banks, and secure safes in all-night convenience stores. It appears that the crime prevention and security technology historically is reactionary to criminal incidents and losses. Only after losses are incurred are improvements made to reduce (or at least change) criminal opportunities. Improved efforts at anticipating changing patterns of theft are needed (see Possamai, 2003; Schuck, 2005).

The dramatic growth in the use and ownership of personal computers during the last twenty years provides another manifestation of new criminal opportunities that were quickly exploited. The invention of the automobile during the early twentieth century has been said to have doubled the number of offenses in the criminal codes of most countries; the invention of the computer likely will have the same effect 100 years later. Automobiles provided opportunities for misuse through untrained operators, manufacturing shortcuts, numerous rules for road usage, complex registration requirements, repair frauds, storage (parking) problems, as well as theft. Computers are having a similar impact as codified offenses are added to eliminate opportunities for misuse such as untrained operators, manufacturing shortcuts, unauthorized usage, registration violations, repair frauds, information storage problems, and theft. Similar to the growth of automobile usage, the growth of computer usage was a threshold event in creating a vast new set of criminal opportunities, which it did not take long to exploit.

The Causes and Prevention of Theft and Fraud

Criminologists try to generalize about why people break the law, although it is has become clear that few adequate generalizations exist to explain criminal conduct such as theft and fraud. Few people steal to survive, and some steal to improve their social standing unlawfully. Some steal to acquire material things they don't actually need, whereas others steal for symbolic reasons involving status, frustration, or revenge. One investigator characterized the causes of fraud in simple terms: "Greed, not misfortune, appears to be the main motivator. Many people think fraudsters are motivated by financial need caused by difficult circumstances—such as illness, divorce, or a financial crisis. However, our research shows such causes are only mentioned in a small number of cases" (Gardham, 2005). Contemporary criminologists focus on external factors (positivism), hedonistic pain/pleasure decisions (classical), political and economic factors (structuralism), and ethics (when criminal decisions bring pleasure rather than shame). These schools of thought are summarized in table 1.3. A full discussion of these approaches to explaining fraud cannot be conducted here, but it can be seen that different explanations may have relevance depending on the circumstances of the case at hand, and that the causes of fraud have direct implications for its prevention.

Table 1.3
Four Approaches to Criminal Behavior

Approach to Crime Causation	Primary Cause of Crime	Prescribed Remedy
Positive	External factors (usually social and economic)	Rehabilitation or reform by changing social and economic conditions, or by changing a person's reaction to them.
Classical	Free-will decision guided by hedonistic tendency to maximize pleasure and minimize pain.	Deterrence through threat of apprehension and punishment.
Structural	Political and economic conditions promote a culture of competitive individualism where personal gain becomes more important than the social good.	More equitable distribution of power and wealth in society, and fewer arbitrary laws, so that all individuals have a greater stake in a better society.
Ethical	Free-will decision guided by ethical principles— illegal conduct occurs because it brings pleasure instead of shame, owing to its wrongfulness and harm to the victim and community.	Education and reinforce ment in ethical decision- making from an early age; reduction to the extent possible the external factors that promote unethical decisions.

Source: Albanese, 2004.

Conclusion

Regardless of the source of offender motivation, history suggests that the enforcement technology will always lag behind the criminal technology. Whether bank safes, credit cards, Internet scams, or other kinds of frauds, criminals have exploited opportunities for theft in a manner that exceeds the existing law enforcement technology. Given changes in the ways we hold, store, and move cash and property, fraud has become an easier, more profitable, and less risky way to steal in the twenty-first century. In addition, the opportunities for fraud are increasing, while the odds of apprehension are not keeping pace, resulting in fraud as a growing crime of choice. Whether efforts to prevent fraud in the twenty-first century will effectively limit opportunities, and also provide quick reactions to changes in the criminal technology, remains to be seen. If history is to be a guide, however, the risk of apprehension must be significantly increased beyond current levels, and the available opportunities more effectively circumscribed.

References

Albanese, Jay *Organized Crime in Our Times*, 4th ed. Lexis/Nexis/Anderson Publishing, 2004.

Associated Press State & Local Wire. "Two Terror Trial Defendants Face New Fraud Charges," December 15, 2004.

Bastian, Lisa D., Patsy Klaus, Craig Perkins, Callie Marie Rennison, and Cheryl Ringel. *Criminal Victimization*. Washington, DC Bureau of Justice Statistics, 2004.

Cressey, Donald R. *Criminal Organization*. New York: Harper & Row, 1972.

Federal Bureau of Investigation. *Crime in the United States*. Washington, DC: U.S. Government Printing Office, 2004.

Fox, Paul D. "Organized Crimes Against Manufacturers and Retailers," *Testimony before U.S. House Judiciary Subcommittee on Crime, Terrorism, and Homeland Security*, (March 17, 2005).

Gardham, Duncan. "Fraud Doubles as Organised Crime Moves In," *The Daily Telegraph (London)*, March 29, 2005.

Holmes, Allan. "Invitation to Steal," *CIO Magazine*, 1 February 2005.

Krebs, Brian. "28 Identity Theft Suspects Arrested in Transatlantic Sting," *The Washington Post*, October 29, 2004, p. E5.

Kirby, Carrie. "New, Smarter Generation of Internet Crooks; Personal-information Thieves Hook Up with People Who May Help Them Profit," *San Francisco Chronicle*, April 11, 2005, p. 1.

McIntosh, Mary. *The Organisation of Crime*. London: Macmillan, 1975.

Jardini, Nancy J. "Money Laundering and Terrorism Financing," Criminal Investigation Internal Revenue Service. *Testimony before U.S. House Financial Services Subcommittee on Oversight and Investigations*. June 16, 2004.

Pankratz, Howard. "10-Year Sentence in 9/11 Scheme," *The Denver Post*, 5 November 2004, p. B4.

Possamai, Mario. "In It for the Long Haul: Cargo Theft Prevention," *Security Management*, vol. 47 (October 2003), p. 93.

Punch, Linda. "The New Fraudsters," *Security*, vol. 17, November 2004, p. 20.

Schuck, Amie M. "American Crime Prevention: Trends and New Frontiers," *Canadian Journal of Criminology and Criminal Justice*, vol. 47 (April 2005), p. 447.

State News Service. "Justice Department Announces 'Operation Roaming Charge' Targeting International and Domestic Telemarketing Fraud," October 5, 2004.

United Nations Interregional Crime and Justice Research Institute. *Trafficking of Nigerian Girls to Italy.* Turin, Italy: United Nations Interregional Crime and Justice Research Institute, 2004.

U.S. Fed News. "Ice Task Force Investigation Leads to Indictment of 26," November 22, 2004.

Warchol, Gregory L. "The Transnational Illegal Wildlife Trade," *Criminal Justice Studies*, vol. 17 (2004), pp. 57-73.

2

Intellectual Property Theft and Organized Crime: The Case of Film Piracy[1]

Jeffrey Scott McIllwain
San Diego State University

Over the past two decades, the industry associations charged with protecting intellectual property industries have aggressively campaigned against intellectual property theft. As part of this campaign, these associations routinely claim that organized crime is a main contributor to the theft of billions of dollars of intellectual property. Their campaigns have been quite successful. High profile investigations of criminal enterprises engaged in these illegal activities have occurred around the world at an ever-increasing rate, resulting in hundreds of thousands of counterfeit items being seized on an annual basis.

The motivation for the receptiveness of governments to take action against intellectual property theft is clearly seen in the United States. Deputy Attorney General Eric H. Holder, Jr. (1999) summarized this motivation. As the U.S. economy transitions from the Industrial Age to the Information Age, he argued, "The United States' economy is increasingly dependent on the production and distribution of intellectual property (IP)." The U.S., "which leads the world in the creation and export of intellectual property and IP-related products," is finding a rapidly increasing portion of its Gross National Product based on intellectual property and its derivatives. Millions of Americans are employed in this sector of the economy, a sector that is experiencing the second greatest rate of job growth in the nation. Given the importance of this sector to the nation's economy, the government, he argues, must protect its interests by making it a

priority to enforce domestic laws and fulfill international treaty obliga-
tions concerning intellectual property theft.

When an economic sector grows as rapidly as this one, it comes as
no surprise that professional criminals look to exploit the opportunities
inherent in it. Since the 1990s, the intellectual property industry has
reportedly lost billions of dollars due to the theft of copyrights, trademarks, and trade secrets. From street level vendors selling counterfeit
items, to workers manufacturing counterfeit goods in sweatshops, and
to bankers and shippers who profit from the trade, an extensive intellectual property shadow economy has developed on a global scale
that mirrors the rapid growth of the legitimate intellectual property
economy. Developments in digital, communication, information, and
transportation technologies have further catalyzed the growth of this
shadow economy, creating even more opportunities for individuals and
groups to enter what they correctly perceive to be a high profit, low risk
criminal enterprise.

Despite this perceived problem, the relationship between organized
crime and intellectual property theft is still virgin territory for criminological research. Indeed, if the databases of the National Institute of
Justice and *Criminal Justice Abstracts* are correct, only one scholarly
article has addressed the subject at all, and it focused on legal instruments used by the state to address the crime, not the crime itself
(Hetzer, 2002). Recognizing this hole in the literature, this article
seeks to understand the processes by which the crime of intellectual
property theft is organized, with specific attention given to film piracy. It seeks to identify the structure and function of the criminal
enterprises engaged in this crime and assess the degree to which
organized crime is involved with film piracy. It does not seek to address the individual level theft of films, like a retiree burning a rented
DVD for his grandchildren or a teenage student illegally downloading a
movie from the Internet.

Definitions

The concept of intellectual property recognizes that individuals
can be granted legal rights over intangible property stemming from
one's intellect and manifest in "novel and unique" ideas. (Task Force
on Intellectual Property, 2004, p. 1). It manifests itself in four legal
areas: copyrights, trademarks, trade secrets, and patents, each of which
is protected to varying degrees by the criminal and civil laws of individual nations.[2]

Intellectual property theft, then, is a generalized term referring to the violation of one of these specific laws. Intellectual property theft is a crime that occurs in both domestic and global contexts. It is also a crime that district, state or national borders cannot contain. As such, there is a need for both domestic and international enforcement mechanisms to address these crimes. When it comes to the piracy of music, film, and software in particular, these domestic and international mechanisms manifest themselves in the public (government) and private (industry associations) sectors.

National laws set forth the specific legal rights of authors, producers, performers, designers, and other creators of intellectual property. However, the lack of standardization in these laws inspired the creation of a number of international treaties concerning intellectual property rights. The most recent of these is the Agreement on Trade-Related Aspects on Intellectual Property Rights (TRIPs). This treaty applies to the 146 World Trade Organization (WTO) countries. TRIPS took effect for developed countries in 1995 and developing countries in 2000. Least-developed countries must comply by 2005 (International Federation of Phonographic Industries, n.d.).[3]

How does one engage in intellectual property theft? The answer to this question provides a large number of variants. Consider a thirteen-year-old boy who illegally downloads his favorite video game from the internet; a covert operative working for a rival nation who infiltrates a major financial institution and steals information on its communications software for the benefit of her country; or a factory owner in a lesser developed part of the world who manufactures counterfeit brand name sunglasses. All of these individuals partake in intellectual property theft of one form or another.

For every type of intellectual theft there are different processes by which the theft occurs. These processes create a vast spectrum of criminal enterprise ranging from the simple to the extraordinarily complex. In some cases, an individual, who otherwise is a model, law-abiding citizen, can engage in it rather simply and with the expenditure of little or no capital (i.e., digitally copying a music CD and giving it to a friend). In other cases, using a substantial amount of investment capital, large transnational networks of professional and semi-professional criminals can work cooperatively to get a stolen product to market (i.e., a major organized crime group manufacturing bogus brand name cigarettes and distributing them to markets in a number of countries).

This study emphasizes the role of organized crime in intellectual property theft, especially film piracy. Since this report centers on the U.S. government's approach to organized crime and intellectual property theft, one must consider the Federal Bureau of Investigation's definition of organized crime:

> ... any group having some manner of a formalized structure and whose primary objective is to obtain money through illegal activities. Such groups maintain their position through the use of actual or threatened violence, corrupt public officials, graft, or extortion, and generally have a significant impact on the people in their locales, region, or the country as a whole (Federal Bureau of Investigation, n.d.).

A statutory definition of organized crime does not exist in the United States. Rather, organized crime is legally referred to as "racketeering," with its many variants defined in the United States Code, Part 1, Chapter 95, § 1961. The most relevant of these definitions refers to that found in 18 U.S.C. 1961 1.b which defines racketeering to be "any act which is indictable under any of the following provisions of title 18, United States Code: ...section 2318 (relating to trafficking in counterfeit labels for phonorecords, computer programs or computer program documentation or packaging and copies of motion pictures or other audiovisual works)....[4]

For the purposes of this study, then, to assess the role of organized crime in the subset of intellectual property theft that is film piracy, one must examine cases where any group having some manner of a formalized structure and whose primary objective is to obtain money through violations of section 2318, and that these groups maintain their position through the use of actual or threatened violence, corrupt public officials, graft, or extortion, and generally have a significant impact on the people in their locales, region, or the country as a whole.

Of course film piracy has its various manifestations. According to the Motion Picture Association (MPA), which coordinates all national motion picture associations, there are eight forms of film piracy: optical disc piracy; internet piracy; videocassette piracy; theatrical print theft; signal theft; broadcast piracy; public performance; and parallel imports. Over the past ten years, the focus of the MPA investigations has been on optical disc piracy [especially Video Compact Discs (VCDs) and Digital Versatile Discs (DVDs)] and, more recently, Internet piracy (Motion Picture Association of America, n.d.). Consequently, these two forms of film piracy form the focus of the ensuing analysis.

Film Piracy

The Motion Picture Association has a very clear position on the relationship between traditional organized crime and film piracy. It exists and it is significant. It came to this conclusion in part due to their unique charge, under international treaties, to investigate intellectual property theft from the motion picture industry, collect data from these investigations, provide the results of their investigations to government officials for arrest and prosecution, and train government officials in how to investigate and prosecute intellectual property theft. The MPA operates field offices and investigations that cover all of the countries that are signatories of the requisite treaties. Since the MPA and its national subsidiaries represent private, not public, concerns, the intelligence they collect and the charges they prepare are considered proprietary information. Consequently, there is a gap between the claims the industry makes concerning the numerous cases of intellectual property theft that occur and the relatively low number of government arrests and prosecutions. The valuable data that composes this gap is, therefore, unavailable for analysis since the associations have no vested interest in making it public beyond very superficial press releases aimed at deterring others from committing similar crimes.

What some of the intellectual property industries do make public are a series of annual reports summarizing, in part or whole, the arrests and prosecutions for the theft of their respective form of intellectual property. Regrettably, when details are provided in these reports, they are anecdotal and of no substantive research value. Consider an example of film piracy found in the report of a U.K.-based intellectual property rights consortium entitled *Proving the Connection*:

International Criminal Network: Triad Gangs and Film Piracy

In December 2002, a piece of investigative journalism by *The People* newspaper uncovered a Triad operation whereby well-known criminal gangs were flooding Britain with pirate DVDs of the latest Harry Potter and James Bond blockbusters, months before their legitimate release for home viewing. The paper's investigators found copies of the DVDs as far afield as London, the West Midlands, Manchester and Nottingham. They reported that the recruits selling the DVDs included Chinese illegal immigrants smuggled in by the Snakeheads Triad group, which traffics people from mainland China (ALLIANCE against Counterfeiting and Piracy, 2002, p. 14).

Putting aside the fact that snakeheads are immigrant smugglers, not a Triad group per se, and the synopsis is based on a press report, not an indictment or other legal proceeding, we are, once again, left with a number of questions: How was the film copied from the original? How was it mass-produced? Who produced it and where was it produced? What capital was expended to fund the operation? How was it distributed to retail agents? How did the retail agents hire their employees? If illegal Chinese immigrants were used as employees, how were they contracted? How much did their services cost? What is the unit cost on the wholesale and retail level? How are customers located and how are they convinced to buy the product? How are the profits of laundered? Are the profits invested in other criminal enterprises? Is participation in the enterprise based on ethnicity, kinship, friendship, or some mixture of the same? Is violence, corruption, graft, etc. ever used to facilitate this enterprise?

In every example given in this report and others, one is left asking similar questions. In all fairness to the associations that produce these reports, they are not meant to serve as data sources for researchers. Indeed, they are actually produced by the public affairs arms of these associations, not the investigative arms. Published industry reports leave us with a number of claims about the relationship between organized crime and film piracy, but little supported fact to back up the assertion.

However, industry claims are buttressed with a tad more detail in government hearings. Testifying before the U.S. House of Representatives on September 23, 2004, John Malcolm, the Senior V.P. and Director of Worldwide Anti-Piracy Operations for the MPA and MPAA, made the following claims: "With rare exceptions, the people procuring, producing, and distributing this pirated material are affiliated with large and dangerous international criminal syndicates." Film piracy is not being operated by "mom-and-pop operations." "It is being done," he stated, "by business-minded thugs who fund this activity through money raised from other illicit activity such as drug dealing, gun running, and human trafficking (utilizing the same distribution networks), and who, in turn, fund these other activities through the money they raise through piracy." Consequently, "…the odds are high that every dollar, pound, peso, euro or rupee spent on them is put into the pockets of bad people who will spend it in a way which is not consonant with our safety and security." Most alarmingly, these groups "have no qualms whatsoever about resorting to violence or bribery to conduct their operations, and they play for keeps," a point he underscores by citing four cases where MPAA investigators were subjected to threats or acts of violence (Malcolm, 2004, September 23).

Speaking a year-and-a-half earlier in his capacity as the Deputy Assistant Attorney General responsible for overseeing the four sections in the Department of Justice's Criminal Division, including the Computer Crime and Intellectual Property Section (CCIPS), Malcolm's comments were more measured, but consistent: "…[O]rganized crime groups are playing a more prominent—and dangerous—role in piracy around the globe," he stated, and is "clearly a factor in global piracy today." He pointed to the experience of one of his CCIPS attorneys who traveled to Malaysia to train Malaysian prosecutors and agents in anti-piracy techniques. These prosecutors and agents told the CCIPS attorney that the production facilities in Malaysia "are owned and operated by organized crime syndicates, specifically very wealthy and powerful criminal groups or Triads from Taiwan which control a significant number of facilities not just in Malaysia but across Asia generally." The CCIPS attorney was then escorted to a large open-air market that offered a variety of pirated products. The attorney learned "that many vendors offer their goods on tables covered in brightly colored cloths which indicate that vendor's affiliation with a specific criminal syndicate" (Malcolm, 2003).

In order to explore these claims further, and with publicly available data either non-existent or unreliable (McIllwain, 2005),[5] an interview of Malcolm was conducted in his office at MPA/MPAA headquarters in Encino, California (Malcolm, 2004, October 8). In a generous gesture, Malcolm also made two key members of his staff, Jim Spertus (2004) and Chad Tilburg (2004), available for interview. Together, they provided the following information about the role of organized crime with optical disc and Internet piracy. Their insight is particularly valuable in that before taking their positions at the MPA and MPAA, Malcolm and Spertus (who is Vice-President and Chief of the MPAA's Domestic Piracy Operations) worked for the Department of Justice and prosecuted intellectual property theft cases. As mentioned previously, Malcolm was the Deputy Assistant Attorney General responsible for the CCIPS and Spertus was a Los Angles-based Deputy U.S. Attorney. Tilburg is considered one of the foremost experts on warez groups and Internet piracy and he provided much needed clarification on the structure and operations of such groups. Unless otherwise noted, the following information comes from interviews with these three men (Malcolm, 2004, October 8; Spertus, 2004; Tilburg, 2004).

Before the interview began, Malcolm made it clear that specifics about the MPA and MPAA investigations were proprietary information. He specifically stated that to do so could compromise investigations currently in progress and possibly endanger his investigators in the field. Despite this, he argued, one can easily draw the conclusion that organized crime was involved with film piracy based on the nature and structure of the enterprise. He and Spertus then provided a step-by-step analysis of how the business of film piracy is conducted. Anecdotes, with key details omitted, were provided to illustrate points. They focused heavily on "hard goods" piracy (optical disc piracy) and "soft goods" piracy (internet piracy). Both of these forms of piracy originated with individuals called "runners."

Runners

The popularity of DVDs created a boom in hard goods piracy, which already had established networks in which pirated videocassettes, software, video games, and music CDs were sold. The flow of DVD piracy begins after the motion picture studio creates the finished product. Individuals with digital video cameras, working independently or in "camcorder rings" and commonly referred to as "runners," attend the first public screenings of these films. These runners use various concealment measures to hide their video cameras with the goal of obtaining the best possible image of the film. Digital sound can be added to the digital image by using the video recorders microphone or, for much higher sound quality, plugging a projector or equipment that assists the hearing impaired directly into the audio input jacks of the digital video camera. In some cases, movie theatre employees are paid to assist and/or protect the runner during the taping process.

The first public screening of a film usually occurs in the New York City area where advanced screenings in theatres with high-end projection and sound systems are common. According to Malcolm, roughly eighty per cent of all pirated films originate from New York City area theaters. This claim is evidenced by the fact that every individual print of a film projected in every individual theater is secretly marked in such a manner that any pirated image can be traced back to the theater in which it was originally projected.

Some runners obtain copies of DVD screeners from motion picture industry sources. A DVD screener is a promotional copy of a film that is created by a movie studio. DVD screeners often contain visible markings to deter piracy, but are still easy to rip if one has the right software. A DVD screener is much preferred over a pirated copy made by a digital video camera because the quality of video and sound is much higher.

Hard Goods Piracy-burners

Once the film is illegally recorded, the runner immediately takes the image home and creates ten to thirty master copies. The master copies are then sold to lab operators for about $100 each. Then the "burning' process begins. Each lab operator uses multiple high-speed DVD burners to make approximately 10,000 copies of a film (the actual number is determined by the anticipated demand for the film). Within 24 hours, anywhere from 100,000 to 300,000 pirated DVDs are available to distributors (in some cases, a lab operator may serve as a distributor). Often times working from warehouses, the distributor packages the DVDs then sells the discs to local or nationwide retail vendors. Retail vendors come in many forms. Some are otherwise legitimate merchants looking to make a profit by selling pirated goods in storefronts, at swap meets, or on internet shopping and auction sites. Other retail vendors are street vendors who either go door-to-door to customers or sell them on the streets.

A street vendor interviewed for this study stated that he purchased new releases from a distributor who used his home as a warehouse. The distributor had a large selection of old and new releases. The street vendor then spent the day walking up-and-down a large section of Whittier Boulevard (a major street in east Los Angeles County), stopping at independently-owned restaurants, auto shops, clothing retailers, gas stations, music shops, mall and supermarket parking lots, parks, and other high traffic locations where a large number of customers tended to congregate. In his case, he targeted customers who spoke his native language (Spanish) and culture (he was from the Mexican state of Michoacan) who were familiar with working with street vendors (not difficult to do given that the area in which he operated has a substantial Mexican immigrant population). He stated that his average profit is about $6 per disc ("Juan," 2004).[6]

The capital outlay for the lab operator depends on the number and quality of computers and DVD burners he or she purchases, as well as all necessary software and the bulk cost of DVR+Rs or DVD-Rs used. Additionally, if the wholesaler or distributor does not do it himself or herself, the lab operator will pay for the cover art and DVD cases. Spertus estimates that the average cost of a wholesale disc, not including packaging, is one dollar. The same disc can then be sold on the streets of New York City for anywhere from $5 to $10 during the week of release. The cost of the disc will then go down as demand decreases in the coming weeks and months.

Success in the optical disc piracy market is based on the following criteria. First, one has to be the "first" in the market. Having the product available the morning or day of its release, if not before, is crucial to earning significant profits. Second, the quality of the packaging needs to be very high because the consumer will equate the quality of the artwork to the quality of the disc in the case. Third, the disc needs to meet certain minimum standards of audio and video clarity so that the customer will purchase future pirated releases.

The creation and distribution of packaging deserves particular attention since it is a very profitable sub-contracting business in its own right. Individual graphic artists make the cover art that slips into the DVD case. They create the cover art in bulk and sell it to the lab owners or distributors. Higher quality cover artwork costs more than lesser quality cover artwork (on average each piece costs approximately ten cents). Since consumers gravitate to products with higher quality artwork, distributors, retailers and consumers are willing to pay more for the most visually enticing and professionally packaged product available.

Hard Goods Piracy-pressers

In addition to selling to domestic lab operators, the runner will also sell master copies to overseas clients. After producing a master copy, the runner will send it by overnight international mail. Once in the possession of the client, the disc is either burned, as discussed above, or pressed. The "pressing" process produces a higher quality DVD than the burning process. The pressing process uses the same DVD replicators that are used by the legitimate DVD production industry to create high quality DVDs. These replicators are either owned by the client (at a cost of approximately $1 million) or are used with the paid-for cooperation of a legitimate DVD production company during off hours.

The idea of the pressed disc is to provide a higher quality alternative to the burned disc. Where it loses out on the profit generated by being the first product in the market, it gains profit by creating a product that, in some cases, nearly equates the quality a legitimately produced product. These clients rely on individuals with considerable video editing skills that "clean up" the original image and re-engineer the sound track to create surround sound. The higher quality DVDs used in this process contain more memory to allow for higher resolution and sound quality. The master is then fed to the replicator that can produce massive amounts of DVDs. In terms of labor, this requires individuals trained to operate the replicators and others who can package the DVDs, using the high quality artwork mentioned above. Because of the higher quality of the disc, the wholesale cost of pressed discs averages between $1 and $2 before packaging.

Produced in countries like Russia, Pakistan, Mexico, Taiwan, Paraguay, Malaysia, Brazil, China, and Thailand, pressed discs are then sent to domestic retailers and exported to international markets. Discs are sent in bulk using standard international shipping methods or they are smuggled into other countries using established smuggling routes and techniques and the professional smugglers who know both.

Soft Goods Piracy

The runner does not just provide a master copy to burning and pressing operations. A master copy will also be sold to a member of a release group, otherwise referred to as a warez (pronounced "wears") group. A warez group specializes in converting a pirated film so that it becomes available to the members of the group and other select clients via the Internet. In addition to pirated film, warez groups also convert pirated software and PC and console (PlayStation 2, Xbox, or Nintendo) video games. According to the Department of Justice:

> Warez release groups are the first-providers - the original source for most of the pirated works traded or distributed online. Once a release group prepares a stolen work for distribution, the material is distributed in minutes to secure, top-level warez servers and made available to a select clientele. From there, within a matter of hours, the pirated works are further distributed throughout the world, ending up on public channels on IRC and peer-to-peer file sharing networks accessible to anyone with Internet access.
>
> The top release groups are hierarchical, highly structured organizations with leadership positions that control day-to-day operations, recruit new members and manage

the group's various computer archive sites. These groups exist solely to engage in piracy and compete with each other to be the first to place a newly pirated work onto the Internet—often before the work is legitimately available to the public. Highly sophisticated technological measures are employed by the groups to shield their illegal activity from victims and law enforcement (Department of Justice, 2004, April).

According to Tilburg (2004) and Spertus (2004), warez groups are not motivated by financial gain. Indeed, getting paid for engaging in piracy results in harsh formal and informal sanctions from the warez community. What motivates warez groups is an enhanced reputation and fame within their peer group, as well as the desire to be the first in the market. There are clear hierarchies in warez groups with distinct divisions of labor. Members of a warez group are almost always known to each other only by their screen names.

The group itself will typically consist of one or two leaders, a council composed of two or three high level members, twelve to fifteen staff members, and a general membership comprising anywhere from twenty to eighty individuals. Leaders have the ultimate authority over their group members. The council members supervise day-to-day operations, "including preparation of new releases, recruitment, and security issues." Staff members are actively engaged in preparing new releases for distribution and in maintaining Top Sites [File Transfer Protocol (FTP) sites] that serve as the point of distribution of pirated products. General warez group members spend a considerable amount of time providing the grunt work for the group, including securing hardware and software needed for group activities and hosting Top Sites (Malcolm, 2003; see also Department of Justice, n.d. b).

Warez groups like to place their own particular stamp of quality on their work and they compete against other warez groups to produce the best product. Entire web pages are dedicated to criticizing and complimenting the work of fellow and rival warez groups and individual group members. Warez groups are extremely security conscious and they use state-of-the-art technology to attempt to prevent police and victim companies from identifying and exposing their illegal activity.

This is not to say that money is not made off of warez group piracy. Pressers have been known to download warez group edited pirated films, video games, and software and use these downloads as the master copies for pressed discs which are then sold for profit. Legitimate businesses also make substantial profits off the work of warez groups. Warez groups will allow certain individuals, referred to as couriers, to ferry content to tightly controlled Top Sites (FTP servers). Access to the Top Site is provided only to trusted parties via websites, newsgroups or peer-to-peer networks. Individuals with access to these Top Sites make the pirated films available to others using Internet Relay Chat (IRC). From there it becomes available to the general public using a variety of mechanisms, including IRC networks like EFNEt, DAL-Net, IRCNEt and Liquid IRC; popular protocols like IRC, eDonkey, Gnutella, Fast Track, Overnet, Bit Torrent, news groups, and the web; and peer-to-peer networks and File Swapping Utilities (FSUs) like KaZaA, Morpheus, eDonkey, Bearshare, eMule, and LimeWire. Money is made when advertisers pay banner providers to place banner ads and popup ads using the services of Top Site Indexers (VCD Quality, NForce), IRC Indexers (PacketNews, XDCC Spy), and Bit Torrent Trackers (Voracity, SuprNova). Banner providers then pay the sites on which they advertise. These sites may also charge users for access to the pirated films on there servers (MediaSentry, Inc., 2003; Spertus, 2004).

As broadband capacity has increased and the cost of hard disc space has decreased, film piracy has boomed on the Internet. It is becoming easier and faster to download films of ever-increasing quality. Indeed, it is so much easier and faster that the motion picture industry is embracing the Internet as a means to deliver their products to legitimate buyers. Of course this same technology can be, and is, used by those engaged in film piracy as well.

Spertus (2004) stated that some optical disc pirates actually use the higher quality warez group produced pirated films as their master copies. Ironically, the proliferation of computers and ever-increasing broadband capacity may actually hurt the optical disc piracy sector, just as it hurts the legitimate motion picture industry. For almost ten years now, Internet savvy consumers have recognized that they can use FSUs like KaZaA and Morpheus to obtain "free" copies of music. Now, movies are becoming ever more popular because the technology exists to make this process easier on the end user. As this technology improves (higher quality pirated films, higher bandwidth, cheaper storage capacity and seamless connectivity to home entertainment systems), the number of pirated films reaching consumers will increase exponentially.

A recent police raid in Iceland underscores this point. With approximately 300,000 residents, Iceland is one of the most "connected" nations in the world, with about 79 percent of its population connected by broadband connections to the Internet. Police raided the homes of twelve people and seized computers and servers used for sharing movie files with the popular DC++ file sharing (P2P) application. According to SMAIS, Iceland's association of film copyright holders that is equivalent to the MPAA in the U.S., net traffic in Iceland dropped 40 percent after these raids were conducted. The implication is clear: 40 percent of Internet traffic in Iceland was dedicated to sharing pirated films. Extrapolate this to global Internet traffic and one can begin to appreciate the magnitude of the theft carried out by these groups (Leyden, 2004; MPAA raids...., Iceland?, 2004).

It should come as no surprise then the Department of Justice has focused some of its major intellectual property operations on investigating and prosecuting warez groups. Operation Buccaneer was one such operation. In December 2001, simultaneous searches were conducted at seventy locations scattered across the U.S., U.K., Australia, Finland, Sweden, and Norway. The investigation targeted multiple top-tier, highly organized and sophisticated warez groups. A number of indictments and convictions resulted (Department of Justice, n.d. a).

The Problem with Government Data

Placing such an investigation like Operation Buccaneer into a larger context is difficult to do since government data on film piracy does not exist. According to the Bureau of Justice Statistics (B.J.S.), the broad category of intellectual property theft was the lead charge in less than 1 percent of all suspects referred to U.S. prosecutors for an intellectual property theft in the nine-year period between 1994 and 2002 (3,395 suspects total) (Motivans, 2002, p. 2). Some of these referrals were handled civilly and others criminally, though the exact proportion is not provided by the B.J.S. U.S. prosecutors did not take action on a substantial number of these referrals, but this portion is also not provided by the B.J.S.[7] The B.J.S. does note that between 100 to 150 people were sentenced each year in U.S. district courts for intellectual property theft offenses between 1995-2002 (Motivans, 2002, p. 4). Such numbers are small given the claims made about the economic costs of intellectual property theft. The Department of Justice Task Force on Intellectual Property recognized this when it recently recommended that the Department needs to do more to generate an increased number of successes when it comes to the investigation and prosecution of intellectual property theft (Task Force on Intellectual Property, 2004, pp. 19-20).

Nevertheless, the vast majority of intellectual property theft cases were addressed through civil remedies. In 2002 alone, 7,445 copyright, patent, and trademark suits were disposed of in U.S. district courts. Of these, however, 76 percent were dismissed. The government was plaintiff or defendant in only thirty-two intellectual property civil cases in 2002 (Motivans, 2002, p. 8).

Since the B.J.S. report also does not provide any information about the involvement of organized crime in intellectual property theft, one needs to sample the criminal cases to which it refers. The presumption here is that if organized crime was involved in a case, it would merit criminal prosecution, not civil action, and that evidence of such activity would appear in indictments and other relevant documents. This presumption is consistent with the Department of Justice's prosecuting guidelines for intellectual property theft (Goldstone, 2001). So the question emerges: What cases does one examine and how does one find them?

This study turned to these cases deemed high profile by the unit that prosecutes them, the Department of Justice's Computer Crime and Intellectual Property Section (CCIPS). This specialized unit was created as a response to industry demands that the government aggressively prosecute intellectual property theft, especially theft of the digital variety. When one looks at the criminal indictments CCIPS deems publicly significant (i.e., generating press releases, summarizing cases on D.O.J. web sites, etc.), one finds a sample of 105 criminal indictments filed from January 2000 to August 2004 (Department of Justice, 2004, August).[8] If organized crime contributes to intellectual property theft, surely, one would reason, these cases would provide us with examples for analysis. Thankfully the Department of Justice lists these cases on its websites dedicated to its efforts in this area (Department of Justice, 2004, August; 2005, April).[9]

Out of the 105 significant cases listed by the Department of Justice (Department of Justice, 2004, August), roughly 70 percent had some form of copyright violation as the leading cause for prosecution. Almost 70 percent of these cases were for violations against the software/hardware industries, 40 percent against the film and music industries (there was overlap between the two in about 15 percent of the prosecutions).

Prosecution by type of violation, total significant cases (N=105):

Copyright[10]	68
Trademark[11]	13
DMCA[12]	3
Unauthorized use of communications[13]	11
Copyright and trademark	6
Copyright and DMCA	2
Unauthorized use of communications and DMCA	1
Money laundering[14]	1

Industry affected by IP crime, total significant cases (N=105):

Film/music:	24
Soft/hardware:	52
Both film/music and soft/hardware:	15
Other/unspecified:	11

However, out of the 105 significant cases listed, less than 50 percent (N=49) were for perpetrator-charged cases. A perpetrator-charged case is when the defendant allegedly operates within a larger, organized framework. Accordingly, these cases deserve the most scrutiny when it comes to looking for connections to organized crime. In perpetrator-charged cases, copyright-related cases composed slightly over 80 percent of the violations charged. A little less than 20 percent were for trademark cases. Once again, prosecutions of intellectual property violations were focused largely on the software/hardware industry (~70 percent) and film and music industry (~35 percent), with some cases overlapping the two industries.

An analysis of the indictments and press releases to these forty-nine perpetrator-charged cases found no overt references to profes-

Prosecution by type of violation, perpetrator charged cases:

Copyright	35
Trademark	5
DMCA	1
Unauthorized use of communications	2
Copyright and trademark	4
Copyright and DMCA	1
Unauthorized use of communications and DMCA	1

Industry affected by IP crime, perpetrator charged cases:

Film/music:	10
Soft/hardware:	26
Both film/music and soft/hardware:	8
Other/unspecified:	5

sional organized crime groups.[15] Instead, the cases were split equally between two broad categories. The first is the "warez". Twenty-one of the forty-nine cases involved prosecutions of individuals in warez groups. Not a single one of these cases, however, asserted the involvement of professional organized crime groups with warez groups.[16]

The second category is one that is composed of twenty-three cases representing a litany of offender types. These include, but are not limited to, companies that made illegal decoders for satellite television boxes, companies and individuals that sold counterfeit business software on eBay or some other forum, and, most interestingly for our purposes, groups of individuals who either produced, distributed or sold bootleg DVDs, CDs, and/or software. As is the case with warez groups, overt references to connections with organized crime groups are non-existent in the CCIPS data. If one does not accept the proposition that warez groups constitute organized crime groups, one cannot find proof of organized crime's involvement with intellectual property theft in this data set.

Film Piracy and Organized Crime

Is organized crime involved with film piracy? The answer to this question is complicated and limited by the lack of reliable data.[17] There are cases where direct links between traditional organized crime groups and optical disc piracy are apparent. The example of Malaysia provided earlier illustrates this point. However, the exact nature of these links needs to be explored further, since information available to the public is anecdotal at best. For example, questions like those that follow need to be answered by independent observers: What specific organized crime groups are involved with this trade? Who are the individuals involved with these groups and how are they connected? Are organized crime groups involved in the entire operation (is the business vertically integrated), or does it focus on certain segments (production, distribution, retail, etc.) or does it just provide "protection" for criminal entrepreneurs? If profits earned from this enterprise aid organized crime groups in other areas, how is this done? For what purposes is this money actually used?

Of course organized crime groups can easily engage in film piracy. If a hypothetical college student can go to Best Buy or Circuit City and purchase a computer, server, software, and disc burners, he can set up a film piracy business rather easily. It stands to reason then that professional criminals, who are always looking to make a quick, easy dollar, can do the same. The opportunity certainly exists for organized crime groups to make considerable profits from film piracy. This opportunity is easily exploited by the fact that organized crime groups are already in the business of operating in the black market, selling products like cigarettes, gasoline, stolen goods, or drugs. Wholesale, distribution and retail channels, as well as transportation, security, and a client base, already exist. Adding pirated goods to the mix makes good financial sense given that the opportunity and motive are so clearly identified.

Given the limited amount of reliable data available, how can the relationship between film piracy and organized crime be assessed? We can begin by applying the criteria established earlier in this study to film piracy groups:

1) Does the group have some formalized structure?
2) Is the primary of objective of the group to obtain money through violations of sections 2318 of the United States Code?
3) Does this group maintain their position through the use of actual or threatened violence, corrupt public officials, graft, or extortion?
4) Does this group generally have a significant impact on the people in their locales, region, or the country as a whole?

Film piracy violates specific racketeering statutes related to intellectual property theft. Consequently, criterion number two is met in every film piracy case. However, the other criteria are more problematic. The first criterion requires a formalized structure on the part of an organized crime group. With the limited amount of data available, we can see where this holds true for some cases of film piracy, especially warez groups, but not others. Indeed, informal structures and fluid (and—in some internet cases—anonymous) networks regularly engage in film piracy. These informal structures and fluid networks can certainly equate criminal conspiracies, but are far from being formal organizations.

To what extent do violence, corruption, graft, and extortion occur in the world of film piracy? Without access to the records of investigators, criterion number three cannot be assessed with any semblance of thoroughness or certainty. There are surprisingly few public cases where violence, corruption, graft and extortion are associated with film piracy, even in the literature produced by intellectual property associations themselves. Those that do exist are woefully lacking in useable data. Indeed, in cases where these activities are evident, organized crime's role in this behavior is often inferred, not proven. In others, it appears that organized crime preyed on those engaged in film piracy, using classic extortion techniques used by professional criminals to "muscle in" on businesses and take a "piece of the action" for themselves.

Some interviews and direct observation of the retail side of film piracy illustrates this process. In June and November 2004 and April 2005 eight retail vendors of pirated DVDs were interviewed at their places of business in Mexico ("Aguilar," 2004; "Beltran," 2004; "Infante," 2004; "Fernandez," 2004; "Mejia," 2005; "Mendoza," 2005; "Negrete," 2004; "Solis," 2004).[18] Six sold pirated DVDs in indoor marketplaces or outdoor markets in major cities ("Ciudad Seca," "Ciudad Alta," and "Ciudad del Norte") and two others sold them in an outdoor flea market in a medium-sized city, "Ciudad de las Tiendas."[19] All of these retailers sold pirated DVDs, VCDs, tapes, software, and videogames from their stalls. All stated that they purchased these products from distributors. They did not produce the goods that they sold. Three of the six retailers in the indoor marketplaces and both of the retailers in the outdoor flea market stated that they pay a protection fee to the "gang" that controlled their respective marketplace (members of these gangs were easily identified as one walked around the marketplaces).

One can conclude that organized crime (if we can elevate the gangs to this status for current purposes) controlled the physical place of business for these retailers, collecting protection payments from not only these merchants but from those who sold legitimate goods as well. The extortion, and the implicit threat of violence this crime entails, that occurred in both places existed as a result of the control of the physical marketplace, not the criminal enterprise of piracy itself. Of course the price of this "protection" was simply passed on to he consumer and viewed by he merchants as a cost of doing business.

Meeting the fourth criterion is easy or difficult, depending on whom one asks. Certainly, in the eyes of the industry and government, piracy groups have a substantial negative impact on the people in their locales, region, or the country as a whole. The industry loses sales and profits and the government loses tax revenue. Additionally, the consumer can be ripped off due to poor audio or image quality. Others, however, would state the impact of piracy has a positive impact on the consumer, who now has inexpensive, if not free, access to films. This holds especially true for those with limited means who cannot afford $12 movie theater tickets or $20 DVDs and never could or would have purchased the ticket or DVD in the first place. Whether or not one views the impact of film piracy as positive or negative, however, the fact that there is a considerable impact is indisputable. The actions of a particular group engaged in film piracy needs to be assessed in this broader context.

Given the criteria, it would be inaccurate to label warez groups as organized crime. Yes they have a formal structure and yes they violate racketeering statutes. They certainly have a considerable impact. Yet they do not engage in violent behavior, extortion, graft, or corruption, cornerstones of any definition of organized crime. Additionally, they are not motivated by profit. As previously discussed, any warez group or member who does work for profit is shunned from the warez community. Indeed, on a certain level, warez groups should be considered a political or ideological action against corporate interests, government power, and globalization that results in criminal behavior. Because of these reasons, warez groups should not be labeled as organized crime groups. Terms like "criminal conspiracy" or "criminal enterprise" are more accurate labels.

Future Concerns

There is no doubt that linking film piracy to organized crime is an effective public relations tool that allows a widely perceived victimless crime to receive the attention and resources of government at a time when other crimes like drugs, money laundering, and terrorism dominate the agenda. If the data were available, one could determine the accuracy of such a claim. Whatever answer one would find is really irrelevant, however, to the main concern and motivation of the motion picture industry. What is really at issue is the future of the revenue patterns on which Hollywood's substantial profits are based.

Until recently, the economics underpinnings of Hollywood were kept even more secret than the data gathered in film piracy investigations. That changed recently when Edward Jay Epstein (2005) published his treatise on the subject, *The Big Picture: The New Logic of Money and Power in Hollywood.* For the first time, a researcher was able to gain access to the Holy Grail of Hollywood: inside information about its accounting and business practices. What he was able to show, despite ardent studio protests to the contrary, was how extremely profitable the motion picture industry actually is, despite numerous claims to the contrary. This includes direct claims made by the MPAA about how, even without factoring in the impact of piracy:

> [m]oviemaking is an inherently risky business. Contrary to popular belief that moviemaking is always profitable, in actuality, only one in ten films ever retrieves its investment from domestic exhibition. In fact, four out of ten movies never recoup the original investment. In 2000, the average major studio film cost $55 million to produce with an extra $27 million to advertise and market, a total cost of over $80 million per film. No other nation in the world risks such immense capital to make, finance, produce and market their films (Motion Picture Association of America, n.d.).

Of course if movie studios only had "domestic exhibitions" to rely on for revenue, the industry as a whole would be in dire straights. Fortunately for the motion picture industry, that is not the case and profits are very high. Central to understanding why these profits are so high, argues Epstein, is to understand that the motion picture industry, as represented by the movie studios, serves the function of a "clearinghouse" for all revenues associated with a particular film. Unlike the revenue system in the old studio system, "in which movies usually returned almost all their money in a year," the revenue for a film "now flows in over the lifetime of licensable rights, which could last for many decades." (Epstein, 2005, p. 110). Since studios do not have a monopoly on these rights (they must contractually share them with producers, directors, actors, writers, music publishers, equity partners, etc.), they must share the revenues with those that have a share in these rights.

As Epstein explains, "when revenue flows in, it is the studio that decides (initially at least) who is entitled to what part of it, and when, and under what conditions." If one of its partners disagrees with the amount of their share, they are at a serious disadvantage. Since the studio is the clearinghouse, "it controls the information on which these payments are based." Of course the studios do their utmost to conceal this information from its partners, concealing "the dimensions of these licensing rights by submerging them in broader, catchall categories in their financial reports." The more effectively the studio conceals this information from outsiders, concludes Epstein:

> the easier it is for the studio to conceal the allocations. Meanwhile, the money that remains in the black box, even temporarily, serves as part of a studio's de facto working capital. The more money the clearinghouse manages to retain, and the longer it retains it, the greater its de facto profit (Epstein, 2005, pp. 110-111).

In order to understand the MPA's concern about film piracy, one has to recognize the importance of intellectual property rights as a central revenue inflow into the clearinghouse. The clearinghouse receives intellectual property payments from the following inflows (Epstein, 2005: pp. 114-116):

- Toy manufacturers, game makers, etc. for rights to use the characters in films. In 2002 alone, entertainment-based characters accounted for over $114 billion in retail sales of licensed products, of which an estimated $1.7 billion went to the studios.
- The movie's box office from the theaters via the studio's distribution arms, with studios collecting on average 45 to 60 percent of the box office.
- Non-theatrical release of a film (airlines' in-flight entertainment, hotel pay-per-view, U.S. military theaters). Airlines and hotels pay a flat fee. Studios collect approximately 50 percent of ticket sales from military theaters.
- Distribution of American films in foreign markets.
- Distribution of foreign films in American markets.
- Video and DVD sales, which accounts for a "tidal wave" of revenue compared to the "small stream" that is the box office. (This accounted for approximately $17.9 billion in revenue in 2003, with $3.9 billion coming from Blockbuster alone.)
- The licensing of a film's television rights, either via pay-per-view or commercial/broadcast television.
- Royalties from record companies from the sale of soundtracks (CDs, cassettes, records) and the songs found on a soundtrack (individual songs purchased and digitally-downloaded from a soundtrack).
- Syndicated television shows also draw substantial licensing fees for studios. (In 2003 the six major Hollywood studios earned an estimated $7.2 billion worldwide from the sale of television programs in their studio libraries.)
- Rebates from various nomenclatures such as film labs also provide a valuable inflow (with up to $800,000 made from a single movie).

Given these inflows, it is inherently difficult to substantiate the value of intellectual property losses by the motion picture industry because stolen intellectual property only gains its value when sold. Indeed, there is no methodology that can prove that the money spent on stolen intellectual property would have been spent on the legitimate intellectual property had the stolen intellectual property not been available. Still, intellectual property theft can feasibly draw away profits from any of the above-mentioned inflows to the clearinghouse. As such, the industry is justified in its concern over the theft of its intellectual property rights as it threatens its revenue streams and profits, especially from DVD sales and rentals (Horn, 2005)[20]

An authoritative, independent study validating the actual claims of losses by the motion picture industry to intellectual property theft, let alone the responsibility of organized crime in that theft, has yet to be published. Building on Epstein's study, the reason is obvious: in order for one to be published, a reliable methodology to determine loss needs to be developed. Once created, the methodology would need to analyze raw data, data that is currently not available to the public in a useable form. This means that the studios would have to make public what they so desperately attempt to conceal—their "clearinghouse" information. So, given current methodological and data constraints, the industry's claims that such losses are excessive, and largely caused by organized crime, are simultaneously unsubstantiated and irrefutable.

Whether or not these losses to intellectual property theft are excessive *right now* is really missing the larger point, however, for it is the *potential of future losses* in a rapidly evolving business and technological environments that concerns the motion picture industry most (Epstein, 2005, pp. 338-352). This evolution is the result of the "digital revolution" in the motion picture industry and the evolution of the "home audience" via "home theater" technologies. Right now, a home entertainment system can be run from a PC that is connected to the Internet via broadband connections. Consumers can watch illegally streamed or downloaded warez group produced films on a high-definition big screen television or computer monitor with surround sound capabilities. Simultaneously, these films can be saved to a hard drive and then recorded to a DVD using a DVD burner and DVD burning software. By doing these things, the consumer can effectively cut the studio out of its income flows from box office sales, cable, broadcast, pay-per-view, DVD and video sales, and rentals, etc.

The only things that prohibit this practice from being more commonplace is the cost of the hardware and software to engage in the activity and, to a lesser extent, bandwidth limitations which can adversely impact the image and sound quality of the film. However, both of these prohibitions are temporary. The cost of home entertainment systems, computer hardware, and computer software continue to decline, making them affordable to the middle and lower classes. Also, as the Internet continues to evolve (increasing exponentially the capacity and efficiency of data transfers), digital media will be available for almost instantaneous download at a much higher level of quality than is currently available. Complicating this situation further is the fact that such technologies and practices have numerous legal, not just illegal, applications. Add to this a generation's worth of consumers, especially youth, who have been educated on computers and the internet and socialized to view illegal downloading as a victimless crime and one can see a formula for future financial turmoil in the motion picture industry.[21] These prospects help us gain a better perspective as to why the motion picture industry and the Department of Justice are largely focusing on warez groups and why they both equate warez groups to organized crime. There is no doubt that these anti-piracy efforts and tactics are about the future, not just the present.

Conclusions

Organized crime is a politically powerful term. To label a person as an organized criminal is to equate them to a cast of real-life and fictitious characters drawn from the gangster tableaux that includes the likes of Al Capone, Meyer Lansky, Pablo Escobar, Vito Corleone, Tony Montana, and Tony Soprano. Linking organized crime to film piracy effectively elevates film piracy in the public's mind to the level of such enterprises as drug trafficking, immigrant smuggling, arms dealing, money laundering, and contract murder. Elevated to this status, it draws the public's attention to a crime that otherwise may be viewed, to the MPA's outrage, as a victimless crime. It certainly seems to have captured the attention of policymakers, who continue to hold hearings on the subject and use the perceived relationship between organized crime (and now terrorism) and film piracy and other forms of intellectual property theft as a basis for stronger legal remedies.

Undoubtedly there are numerous criminal entrepreneurs who produce, distribute, and sell stolen films for profit at swap meets, bazaars and market places around the globe. Yet these criminal entrepreneurs are not organized criminals just because they engage in film piracy. They are only organized criminals when they meet the long-held criteria established in the law and in the application of the law by police and prosecutorial organizations, criteria that encompass such actions as violence and corruption. Unless this occurs, they are more accurately labeled criminal entrepreneurs, criminal enterprises, or racketeers.

How many film pirates meet these criteria? This is an unanswerable question based on the available data. The role of organized crime in film piracy may be extensive. It may not. Organized crime may manifest itself in film piracy in a number of ways in a number of different locales around the world. However, it may be remarkably consistent in its manifestations wherever it is found. International crime syndicates may have vertically integrated control of film piracy in some markets. Then again, a particular group may just be involved in a particular segment of film piracy (e.g., smuggling) at a given place during a given time. The inability to come to basic conclusions about the relationship of organized crime to film piracy results from a profuse lack of useable and verifiable information in media, government and industry sources.

In the absence of independent, substantive analysis, anecdote and industry interests currently drive public policies and legal developments created to address the role of organized crime in film piracy. Nonetheless, this is not to say that such policies and laws are misdirected, ineffective or unnecessary. Indeed, recent efforts to strengthen both have paid considerable dividends for the intellectual property industries as a whole. In the U.S. and across the globe, seizures, criminal indictments, civil actions, and public awareness are up considerably. Whether or not these advances can be maintained in the face of technological advances, the evolution of industry economic structures, and consumer indifference to the stigma of intellectual property theft and anger at industry responses to such theft remains to be seen.

In order to obtain an independent and substantive analysis of the relationship of organized crime to intellectual property theft in general and film piracy in particular, the National Institute of Justice and other grant agencies should consider funding the following paths of research:

1) The development of a methodology to provide an accurate assessment of industry claims of losses to intellectual property theft.
2) The development of a database with data (actors, activities, etc.) drawn from adjudicated criminal and civil cases. This database should collect information on the international level.
3) Ethnographic research of intellectual property theft.
4) Interviews and surveys of convicted intellectual property thieves.

5)   Interviews and surveys of the consumers of stolen intellectual property.

Pursuing these paths of research would allow for the development of research models for situations in which there is a vague, suspected, or otherwise undocumented relationship between a criminal activity and the suspected perpetrators. These models would then, in turn, provide for a more efficient and effective allocation of government and public resources as they attempt to address these types of crime.

Notes

1.   The author would like to thank the International Center of the National Institute of Justice for funding this research through a grant, Intellectual Property and Organized Crime. He also thanks Jay Albanese and the anonymous reviewers of this work for their helpful comments and criticisms. This article only reflects the findings of the author, not the National Institute of Justice, Dr. Albanese or the reviewers.

2.   Specifically, the following crimes have been codified in the United States Criminal Code *Copyright:* Criminal Infringement of a Copyright; Trafficking in Counterfeit Labels of Phonograph Records, Copies of Computer Programs, and Similar Materials; Unauthorized Fixation of and Trafficking in Sound Recordings and Music Videos of Live Musical Performances; Unauthorized Reception of Cable Services; and Unauthorized Publication or Use of Communication. *Trademark:* Trafficking in Counterfeit Goods or Services. *Trade Secrets:* Economic Espionage and Theft of Trade Secrets.

3.   The TRIPs agreement requires all members to comply with established treaties that establish a list of rights for provided to authors, producers and composers, including the rights to authorize or prohibit reproduction, public communication, or adaptation of their works. TRIPS also provides a specific right to authorize or prohibit commercial rental of these works and a detailed set of requirements relating to the enforcement of rights which, in sum, requires remedies and procedures to effectively deter piracy. Soon after the TRIPs agreement, the international community adopted two treaties in 1996 under the auspices of the World Intellectual Property Organization (WIPO) of the United Nations. The WIPO Copyright Treaty is applicable to authors and the WIPO Performances and Phonograms Treaty (WPPT) is applicable to performers and phonogram producers. These treaties brought copyright protection to the digital age by granting rights with respect to distribution activities over computer programs; protecting against unauthorized internet use; protecting technological measures used on copyright material and rights-management information against hacking, removal or alteration. A full-scale review of TRIPs is currently underway and it will reveal the shortcomings of TRIPs in the view of technological agreements.

4.   The full text reads as follows: United States Code, Title 18, Part 1, Chapter 113, § 2318: Trafficking in counterfeit labels for phonorecords, copies of computer programs or computer program documentation or packaging, and copies of motion pictures or other audio visual works, and trafficking in counterfeit computer program documentation or packaging.
(a) Whoever, in any of the circumstances described in subsection (c) of this section, knowingly traffics in a counterfeit label affixed or designed to be affixed to

a phonorecord, or a copy of a computer program or documentation or packaging for a computer program, or a copy of a motion picture or other audiovisual work, and whoever, in any of the circumstances described in subsection (c) of this section, knowingly traffics in counterfeit documentation or packaging for a computer program, shall be fined under this title or imprisoned for not more than five years, or both.

(b) As used in this section—

(1)   the term "counterfeit label" means an identifying label or container that appears to be genuine, but is not;

(2)   the term "traffic" means to transport, transfer or otherwise dispose of, to another, as consideration for anything of value or to make or obtain control of with intent to so transport, transfer or dispose of; and

(3)   the terms "copy," "phonorecord," "motion picture," "computer program," and "audiovisual work" have, respectively, the meanings given those terms in section 101 (relating to definitions) of title 17.

(c) The circumstances referred to in subsection (a) of this section are—

(1)   the offense is committed within the special maritime and territorial jurisdiction of the United States; or within the special aircraft jurisdiction of the United States (as defined in section 46501 of title 49);

(2)   the mail or a facility of interstate or foreign commerce is used or intended to be used in the commission of the offense;

(3)   the counterfeit label is affixed to or encloses, or is designed to be affixed to or enclose, a copy of a copyrighted computer program or copyrighted documentation or packaging for a computer program, a copyrighted motion picture or other audiovisual work, or a phonorecord of a copyrighted sound recording; or

(4)   The counterfeited documentation or packaging for a computer program is copyrighted.

(d) When any person is convicted of any violation of subsection (a), the court in its judgment of conviction shall in addition to the penalty therein prescribed, order the forfeiture and destruction or other disposition of all counterfeit labels and all articles to which counterfeit labels have been affixed or which were intended to have had such labels affixed.

(e) Except to the extent they are inconsistent with the provisions of this title, all provisions of section 509, title 17, United States Code, are applicable to violations of subsection (a).

5.   Please contact the author for a copy of this unpublished report (mcillwai@mail. sdsu.edu).

6.   "Juan" is a pseudonym used to protect the identity of the source.

7.   "The most common reasons provided by U.S. attorneys for declining to prosecute in 2002 were weak/insufficient admissible evidence (20 percent), agency request (17 percent), lack of evidence of criminal intent (12%), and civil/administrative action/prosecution by other authorities (11 percent)" (Motivans, 2002, p. 4).

8.   As stated on this CCIPS web site, this is a representative, not exhaustive, sample of prosecuted cases. This is the most comprehensive summary of such cases available to the public. Note that when translating the information found on "Computer Crime and Intellectual Property Section (CCIPS) Intellectual Property Cases" summary, one case was dropped. *U.S. v. Sama et al.* is listed twice, so it is only counted once throughout the summary found in this report.

9.   This has even more merit for future cases since the Department of Justice Task Force on Intellectual Property recently recommended that DOJ "Target Large, Complex Criminal Organizations That Commit Intellectual Property Crimes" (Task Force on Intellectual Property, 2004, pp. 19-20).

10.   Copyright: 18 U.S.C. § 2318 and 2319 prohibit, respectively, trafficking in counterfeit labels and documentation, and infringing a copyright.
11.   Trademark: 18 U.S.C. § 2320 bans trafficking in counterfeit goods or services.
12.   Digital Millennium Copyright Act: 17 U.S.C. § 1201prohibits the circumvention of copyright protection systems.
13.   Unauthorized use of communications: 47 U.S.C. § 605 bans the unauthorized use of telecommunications services (such as satellite television programming) as well as the distribution of devices that enable such unauthorized use.
14.   The Department of Justice does not specify the specific statute violated when it refers to money laundering.
15.   Professional organized crime groups as defined earlier in the paper. Connections, or lack thereof, to such groups were determined through indictments and press releases associated with the cases provided on D.O.J.'s "Computer Crime and Intellectual Property Section (CCIPS) Intellectual Property Cases" summary (Department of Justice, 2004, August) and a search of on-line search engines for information about each indictment.
16.   There was also one case of a hacker being charged. It is not included in the warez classification provided here.
17.   When one searches through media coverage of intellectual property theft (in this case using LexisNexis), a number of stories emerge. However, the coverage is very far from comprehensive, telling the reader an arrest, prosecution or sentencing of intellectual property thieves has occurred, but offering little to no information that would lend itself to a substantive analysis. The following story, "Annual Cost of Film Piracy Put at Pounds 400M and Rising as More Copies Are Seized" from *The Independent* (2003) is representative:

"Film piracy in Britain allegedly increased by 80 percent last year, costing the motion picture industry pounds 400m in lost sales. The pirates' stranglehold was demonstrated when fake DVDs of the second *Tomb Raider* movie *The Cradle of Life* were discovered on sale on British streets days before the film is premiered tomorrow. Officials from the U.K. Film Council found DVDs of *The Cradle of Life* for sale for pounds five each in Oxford Street, London. A spokesman said: 'They were shocking quality and there was no sound for at least the first five minutes.' Seizures in 2002 were double those of the previous year, with 659,000 illegal copies recovered worth a potential pounds 10m. Illegal copies are often sold by dealers at car boot fairs and street markets. They are packaged to look like the real thing but often suffer from poor sound, colour and clarity. UK successes such as *Bend it like Beckham*, *Gosford Park* and *28 Days Later* have all been copied by pirates while Hollywood hits *The Hulk*, *Terminator 3* and *Pirates of the Caribbean* have been on the streets before a cinema release. About one in three videos bought is believed to be an illegal copy. They can usually be spotted because they have no BBFC classification, and are said to often fund crime syndicates. The U.K. Film Council has set up a task force, which intends to map out the extent of the problem and find long-term solutions, such as toughening the law. Mr. Green said: 'More than 50,000 people work in the U.K.'s film and video sector and piracy is a direct attack on their jobs and our economy generally, inhibiting the growth of our own industry.' John Woodward, the chief executive of the U.K. Film Council, said: 'People need to remember that when they buy a pirate DVD or video they are not only likely to end up wasting their money on a poor quality product, they are often putting money straight into the hands of organised criminals. Cheap copies from markets and car boot fairs may seem a bargain, but in the long-run we all lose out.'"

The story's structure is quite formulaic, most seemingly based on the press release of a government agency or industry association. The structure of the story usually reads as follows: Pirated copies of recent releases are being found on the streets in ever-increasing quantities. It costs the motion picture industry millions of dollars in losses. Consumers are getting ripped-off by the inferior quality of the counterfeit product. This is how you identify a fake product. Proceeds from this crime fund organized crime that endangers society. This crime hurts the motion picture industry, thereby costing jobs.

The problem with such reports is that they are of little to no value to the researcher. They are full of unsubstantiated claims (i.e., "People need to remember that when you buy a pirate DVD or video they are...often putting money straight into the hands of organized criminals.") The claims may be true, but where is the hard evidence? Additionally, the stories have the central purpose of persuading the reader not to buy pirated products, rather than providing a thorough analysis of how intellectual property theft actually equates or works with organized crime.

18.   All of these names are pseudonyms used to protect the identity of the sources.

19.   All city names are pseudonyms used to protect the identity of the sources.

20.   Based on this report, once con conclude that the motion picture industry generally guards DVD information as if it was the Holy Grail itself. With 2004 domestic DVD sales reaching approximately $15.5 billion and DVD rentals grossing $5.7 billion (compared to domestic theater ticket sales which totaled $9.5 billion the same year), one can see why these numbers are withheld for the financial advantage of the studios. A number of lawsuits, including one from Peter Jackson, director of the *Lord of the Rings* trilogy, accuse movie studios of hiding the actual number and timing of DVD sales, thereby preventing accurate residual payments to film stakeholders.

21.   Illustrating this point is the informal, unscientific survey the author took of 104 undergraduate and graduate students, most of whom were criminal justice majors. When asked if they have ever illegally downloaded music or film from the internet, ninety-nine responded yes. When asked why they illegally downloaded the music, the two overwhelming responses were "it's free" and "cd's cost too much" (ninety-five total responses).

References

"Aguilar." (2004). Interview with Jeffrey McIllwain. "Ciudad Seca," Mexico.

ALLIANCE against Counterfeiting and Piracy. (2002). *Proving the connection: Links between intellectual property theft and organised crime*. Retrieved May 1, 2005 from www.aacp.org.uk/Proving-the-Connection.pdf and http://66.102.7.104/search?q=cache: Ipm92QjC4IoJ:www.aacp.org.uk/Proving-the-Connection.pdf+proving+the+ connection&hl=en&client=firefox-a. : 14.

Annual cost of film piracy put at pounds 400M and rising as more copies are seized. (2003, August 18). *The Independent*. Retrieved May 1, 2005 from LexisNexis Academic.

"Beltran." (2004). Interview with Jeffrey McIllwain. "Ciudad Alta," Mexico. Department of Justice. (2004, April 22). Justice Department announces international Internet piracy sweep. Retrieved May 1, 2005 from http://www.usdoj.gov/opa/pr/2004/April/04_crm_263.htm.

Department of Justice. (2004, August). Computer Crime and Intellectual Property Section (CCIPS) intellectual property cases. Retrieved May 1, 2005 from http://www.usdoj.gov/criminal/cybercrime/ipcases.htm.

Department of Justice. (2005, April 15). Computer Crime and Intellectual Property Section (CCIPS) Protecting Intellectual Property Rights: Copyrights, Trademarks and Trade Secrets. Retrieved May 1, 2005 from http://www.usdoj.gov/criminal/cybercrime/ip.html.

Department of Justice. (n.d. a). Operation Buccaneer. Retrieved May 1, 2005 from http://www.usdoj.gov/criminal/cybercrime/ob/OBMain.htm.

Department of Justice. (n.d. b). Operation Buccaneer: Illegal warez operations and Internet piracy. Retrieved May 1, 2005 from http://www.usdoj.gov/criminal/cybercrime/ob/OBorg&pr.htm.

Epstein, E. J. (2005). *The Big Picture: The New Logic of Money and Power in Hollywood.* New York: Random House.

Federal Bureau of Investigation. (n.d.). Organized crime glossary. Retrieved May 1, 2005 from http://www.fbi.gov/hq/cid/orgcrime/glossary.htm.

"Fernandez." (2004). Interview with Jeffrey McIllwain. "Ciudad de las Tiendas," Mexico.

Goldstone, D. (2001, March). Deciding whether to prosecute an intellectual property case. *USA Bulletin.* Retrieved May 1, 2005 from http://www.usdoj.gov/criminal/cybercrime/usamarch2001_1.htm.

Hetzer, W. (2002). Godfathers and pirates: Counterfeiting and organized crime. *European Journal of Crime Criminal Law and Criminal Justice* 10:4, pp. 303-320.

Holder, E. (1999, July 23). "Remarks of Eric H. Holder, Jr., Deputy Attorney General, U.S. Department of Justice, at a Press Conference Announcing the Intellectual Property Rights Initiative, San Jose, California." Retrieved May 1, 2005 from www.usdoj.gov/criminal/cybercrime/dagipini.htm.

International Federation of Phonographic Industries. (n.d.). "Copyright and related-rights treaties and laws." Retrieved May 1, 2005 from http://www.ifpi.org/site-content/legal/treaties.html.

"Infante." (2004). Interview with Jeffrey McIllwain. "Ciudad Alta," Mexico.

Horn, J. (2005, April 17). DVD sales figures turn every film into a mystery. *Los Angeles Times.*

"Juan." (2004, August 17). Interview with Jeffrey McIllwain. Whittier, California.

Leyden, J. (2004, September 30). Iceland's net traffic plummets, following P2P raids. *The Register.* Retrieved May 1, 2005 from http://www.theregister.co.uk/2004/09/30/p2p_raids_iceland/.

Malcolm, J. G. (2003, March 13). Statement of John G. Malcolm, Deputy Assistant Attorney General. Hearing on Copyright Piracy and Links to Crime and Terrorism, Subcommittee on the Courts, The Internet, and Intellectual Property, Committee on the Judiciary, U.S. House of Representatives. Retrieved May 1, 2005 from LexisNexis Academic.

Malcolm, J. G. (2004, September 23). Statement of John G. Malcolm, Jr., Sr. V.P. & Director Worldwide Anti-Piracy Operations Motion Picture Association of America. Hearing on Protecting U.S. Innovations from Intellectual Property Piracy, Committee on Government Reform, U.S. House of Representatives. Retrieved May 1, 2005 from LexisNexis Academic.

Malcolm, J.G. (2004, October 8). Interview with Jeffrey McIllwain. Encino, California.

McIllwain, J. S. (2005). Organized crime and intellectual property theft. Unpublished report for the International Center, National Institute of Justice.

MediaSentry, Inc. (2003). Movie piracy flow. Unpublished document provided to the author by Jim Spertus (2004).

"Mejia." (2005). Interview with Jeffrey McIllwain. Mexico. "Ciudad del Norte," Mexico.

"Mendoza." (2005). Interview with Jeffrey McIllwain. Mexico. "Ciudad del Norte," Mexico.

Motion Picture Association of America. (n.d.) "Anti-Piracy". Retrieved May 1, 2005 from http://www.mpaa.org/anti-piracy/.

Motivans, M. (2004, October). Intellectual Property Theft, 2002. *Bureau of Justice Statistics Special Report.* Retrieved on May 1, 2005 from http://www.ojp.usdoj.gov/bjs/abstract/ipt02.htm.

MPAA raids ... Iceland? (2004, October 1). BroadbandReports.com. Retrieved May 1, 2005 from http://www.broadbandreports.com/shownews/55034.

"Negrete." (2004). Interview with Jeffrey McIllwain. "Ciudad Seca," Mexico.

"Solis." (2004). Interview with Jeffrey McIllwain. "Ciudad de las Tiendas," Mexico.

Spertus, J. (2004, October 8). Interview with Jeffrey McIllwain. Encino, California.

Task Force on Intellectual Property. (2004). *Report of the Department of Justice's Task Force on Intellectual Property.* Washington, DC: United States Department of Justice.

Tilburg, C. (2004, October 8). Interview with Jeffrey McIllwain. Encino, California.

3

Causes and Prevention of Intellectual Property Crime

Nicole Leeper Piquero
University of Florida

Introduction

Intellectual property refers to any product that results from the creativity and innovation of the human mind and the original expression of those ideas (Stim, 2000; Ronkainen and Guerrero-Cusumano, 2001; Luckenbill and Miller, 1998). In other words, intellectual property covers just about every possible idea or invention from the arts and literary fields (i.e., books, photographs, recordings, choreography, etc.) to science and technology. Intellectual property right laws in the U.S. grant the exclusive ownership and rights to use, produce, and distribute creative work to the creator or author.

According to the World Intellectual Property Organization (WIPO), "intellectual creation is one of the basic prerequisites of all social, economic, and cultural development" (WIPO, 2001, p. 41). Therefore, the absence of laws and regulations governing the rights of individuals to freely create and develop innovations may stymie technology, cultural, and intellectual advancements. So why is the protection of intellectual property so important? Does it matter if the production of ideas and innovations slows to a snail's pace or stops all together? Intellectual property is believed to form the backbone of economic activity and give a competitive advantage in the world marketplace particularly to industrialized nations (Ronkainen and Guerrero-Cusumano, 2001, p. 59). In the U.S., copyright industries rather consistently account for approximately 5 percent of the country's Gross Domestic Product (GDP). In order to protect economic interest and promote innovation and advancement, it is important to protect intellectual property from piracy and theft.

However, some in the legal arena disagree and argue that the obsessive American concern with protecting intellectual property is counterproductive and oppressive in various ways (see Lessig, 2001). Additionally, other legal scholars have addressed many important matters of relevance designed to produce a more complete understanding of intellectual property rights and violations such as the intersection of freedom of speech and intellectual property rights (Yen, 2003; Volokh, 2003), the challenge to preserve works that are created in a digital format while not violating the exclusive rights of the copyright owner (Gasaway, 2003), the role of applying criminal laws to copyrighted material and how the imposition of these laws can stifle creativity and reduce innovation (Moohr, 2003), the creation of the "copyleft"—an anti-law movement that emphasizes the free availability of art (Dusollier, 2003), as well as the implication of intellectual property issues in an international context (Endeshaw, 2002; Patry, 2003; Story, 2003). Although these efforts have certainly provided important evidentiary background regarding the legal issues associated with intellectual property rights, they have offered little help in understanding the social science assessment of the causes and prevention efforts of intellectual property violations.

There are generally four recognized types or categories of intellectual property: copyright, patents, trademarks, and trade secrets. Copyrights deal largely with forms of creativity concerning mass communications such as novels, music, song lyrics, motion pictures, plays, computer programs, and choreography to list a few examples (WIPO, 2001, p. 40). Patents are used to protect new inventions so that they cannot be exploited or used without the authorization of the patent owner (WIPO, 2001, p. 17). Trademarks are designed to individualize goods and services (referred to as service marks) in order for consumers to distinguish the source (Poltorak and Lerner, 2002). A trademark can be a symbol, a word, a design, a logo, a slogan, or any combination thereof that distinguishes one brand from another. Trade Secrets refer to business information that is kept in confidence such as formulas, patterns, devices, strategies, and techniques that are used to obtain and advantage over competitors (Stim, 2000).

Violations of intellectual property rights have long been an issue receiving at least some attention but the level of attention has been ratcheted up considerably in recent years. Of course, the real challenge is to understand why "copying" as a form of theft—a view widely held by copyright holders—is not more widely shared by members of the public. Through a series of high profile lawsuits (*RIAA v. John Does*; *A&M Records v. Napster*; *RIAA v. Napster*; *Metallica v. Napster*) the music and motion picture industries have recently raised the general awareness of copyright violations. The copying of computer software, movies, video games, and music deny publishers and authors' economic returns on their property and with the adaptations constantly being made to the definition of "property" this really amounts to nothing more than theft (Carruthers and Ariovich, 2004). Unfortunately, despite the increased attention, very little is actually known about the extent of the problem; the costs associated with the misuse and theft of intellectual property; the causes of intellectual property theft; the policy responses to intellectual property violations; and the effectiveness of existing responses. The current research attempts to fill this void by providing a review of the current state of research regarding these issues, as well as outlining an agenda for future research.

Nature and Extent of Intellectual Property Theft

Though the rights of intellectual property are related to and oftentimes suggested to be similar to the ownership of other forms of physical property (e.g., tangible property), there are several unique features of intellectual property that separate it from tangible property (Seale, Polakowski, and Schneider, 1998). First, there is a nonexclusive dimension of intellectual property. Unlike tangible goods, intellectual property is not consumed by its use. In other words, intellectual property can be used in many places at once. Computer software provides a perfect illustration of intangible property that does not need to be removed from the owner's possession in order to be useful to another (Thong and Yap, 1998). With the theft of tangible property the owner is deprived of the use of his or her property but this is not the case with the theft of intellectual property. Hence, the nonexclusive nature of intellectual property makes it harder to maintain exclusive use over intellectual property than it is to control tangible property (Seale et al., 1998, p. 29). Second, retail costs rarely reflect production costs (Seale et al., 1998). Since perceptions of price and value matter to consumers (Zeithaml, 1988), a sense of unfairness may surface when faced with a discrepancy between manufacturing costs and purchase price (Seale et al., 1998). This sense of unfairness matters to the point that consumers believe they are getting their money's worth. When consumers believe that they are paying more than what is deserved for a desired good (or service), the perceived unfair price may become the needed motivation to find cheaper ways to obtain the product, including piracy. Finally, many forms of intellectual property theft require skills and expertise as well as opportunity to offend (Seale et al., 1998). Unlike tangible property, the theft of many (but not all) forms of intellectual property requires a certain level of skill and know-how, such as how to use a computer or how to navigate the internet, as well as exposure to equipment (i.e., computer) to aid in the theft. While it is assumed that opportunities for street crimes (e.g., theft of tangible property) are generally available to everyone (Gottfredson and Hirschi, 1990; Cohen and Felson, 1979), the same is not true with regard to intellectual property theft—not everyone possesses the skills nor has the opportunity readily available to engage in intellectual property theft. This last feature is important in that it limits who is capable of engaging in intellectual property theft.

Similarities are drawn between tangible property and intellectual property theft in order to explain the behavior in familiar terms. In some instances the law is able to change and adapt in order to incorporate new forms of intangible property under its purview. For example, property now includes intangibles such as bonds, shares, trademarks, and patents (Carruthers and Ariovich, 2004). However, the relevance of the unique features of intellectual property cannot be overlooked. They matter to the point that it is hard for the public to not only comprehend that a theft has occurred—after all no tangible product has been taken; but, also to the point that the public becomes outraged at such behavior. Once the public becomes outraged, it becomes a social problem that needs to be addressed and corrective actions can be put into place to prohibit the behavior. Up until now, those most likely to abhor the behavior are those who would benefit from its protection. Business groups and trade associations such as the Business Software Alliance (BSA), the Recording Industry Association of America (RIAA), and the Motion Picture Association of America (MPAA) are lobbying the government to become more involved in protecting intellectual property rights domestically and abroad (Carruthers and Ariovich, 2004).

Because the breadth of intellectual property is so wide, it is diffi-cult to obtain precise measurements as to how much theft is actually occurring. Luckenbill and Miller (1998) suggest that the quantity of intellectual property at least in the U.S. has considerably increased over the past century. By examining the number of pieces of intel-lectual property (i.e., copyrights, patents, and trademarks) registered annually with the U.S. federal government, they concluded that the increase over the past century has been roughly on the order of four to five times more pieces of intellectual property (Luckenbill and Miller, 1998, p. 94). This growth in volume, they suggest, has allowed intellectual property to become more vulnerable to misuse. The latest developments in technology allow for easy duplication with minimal flaws (Christensen and Eining, 1991). Therefore, copyrighted materi-als have been the easiest targets.

Estimating the costs of intellectual property theft also is not an easy task. Each industry calculates its own losses, but one thing is certain: across all industry estimates, the losses incurred are significant. In 1997, the U.S. theft of intellectual property rights were estimated to cost $300 billion with high technology corporations the most frequently targeted (Maher and Thompson, 2002). The music industry places the value of the sales of pirated recordings at $4.6 billion for 2002, an increase of 7 percent from the proceeding year (IFPI, 2003). The motion picture industry estimates that $1.25 billion were lost between 1998 and 2002 due to audiovisual piracy (not including the impact on internet piracy nor losses stemming from signal theft) in the U.S. alone (MPA, 2003). Meanwhile, worldwide estimates on the annual dollar amount of software pirated range anywhere from $7.5 to $17 billion (Ronkainen and Guer-rero-Cusumano, 2001; Christensen and Eining, 1991, p. 68). Regardless, one overall conclusion, made recently by the Office of the U.S. Trade Representative 2004 Annual "Special 301" report, is that the lack of intellectual property rights protection and enforcement continues to be a global problem.

Since industrialized nations are believed to most benefit from intel-lectual property rights protection, it should come as no surprise that the U.S. government has been particularly instrumental in pushing for international protections for intellectual property rights (USTR, 2004). The U.S. government works closely with the World Trade Or-ganization (WTO), an international organizational designed to deal with the rules of trade between nations, in order to ensure that WTO members adhere and uphold the rules established by the Trade-Related Aspects of Intellectual Property Rights (TRIPS) by providing extensive technical assistance and training on implementing the TRIPS agreement. This agreement established in 1994 set forth rules to govern the rights of intellectual property as part of worldwide trade negotiations such as requiring a minimum standard of protection for many forms of intellectual property (i.e., patents, copyrights, trademarks, trade secrets, geographical indicators), providing effective enforcement of these rights, and allowing disputes to be settled through the WTO's dispute settlement mechanism (Carruthers and Ariovich, 2004; USTR, 2004).

The Office of the U.S. Trade Representative (USTR) annually reports on the adequacy and effectiveness of intellectual property rights protection with the countries that serve as trading partners to the U.S. They monitor and categorize countries that are not complying with the TRIPS regulations. Fifty-two countries have been designated as either Priority Foreign Countries, Priority Watch List, Watch List, or those that fall under Section 306 monitoring. Priority Foreign Countries are those that have the most onerous and egregious policies that have the greatest adverse impact on relevant U.S. products and who are not involved in good faith negotiations to make significant progress in addressing these problems (USTR, 2004). These countries are subject to intense investigation and possible sanctions. Only Ukraine made the Priority Foreign Countries list. Countries are placed on the Priority Watch List when they do not provide an adequate level of intellectual property rights protection and enforcement or market access for persons relying in intellectual property protection. Fifteen countries were placed on the Priority Watch List (Argentina, Bahamas, Brazil, Egypt, European Union, India, Indonesia, Korea, Kuwait, Lebanon, Pakistan, Phillippines, Russia, Taiwan, and Turkey). Thirty-four countries made the Watch List indicating that they merit bilateral attention to address the underlying intellectual property right problems they face. These countries include: Azerbaijan, Belarus, Belize, Bolivia, Canada, Chile, Colombia, Costa Rica, Croatia, Dominican Republic, Ecuador, Guatemala, Hungary, Israel, Italy, Jamaica, Kazakhstan, Latvia, Lithuania, Malaysia, Mexico, Peru, Poland, Romania, Saudi Arabia, Slovak Republic, Tajikistan, Thailand, Turkmenistan, Uruguay, Uzbekistan, Venezuela, and Vietnam. Finally, two countries fall under the category of Section 306 monitoring, China and Paraguay, because of serious intellectual property problems and previous bilateral agreements reached with the U.S. to address specific problems. From this report one thing is clear: the U.S. government is keeping a close eye on the steps and efforts taken by foreign countries in order to help protect the intellectual property rights of U.S. products.

With this background in hand, the next section outlines a series of different theoretical explanations that have been put forth to account for intellectual property violations.

Causes of Intellectual Property Theft

In order to understand and combat the theft of intellectual property, it is important to examine the underlying motivations and justifications of such behavior. Most research seeking to understand the causes of the behavior are limited to the violation of copyright realm of intellectual property theft with an even more specific focus on software piracy. Despite the narrow definition of intellectual property, much insight can be gained by understanding the motivation and reasoning behind this specific form of intellectual property theft. The opportunities to offend are first discussed followed by different theoretical models that have been used to explain the theft of intellectual property.

Opportunity to Offend

Advances in information technology have not only provided worldwide access to creative works for the consuming public but have also posed a serious threat to authors of copyrighted material (Luckenbill and Miller, 1998). With each passing decade, new technological advances created challenges for the protection of intellectual property (Luckenbill and Miller, 1998). The proliferation of photocopying machines throughout the 1960s raised copyright concerns for literary field with regards to published materials such as journal articles and novels. The 1970s ushered in the era of the personal computer and home video (e.g., VCR) posing serious threats to the software and the motion picture industry. Digital audiotape recorders threatened the music industry throughout the 1980s while the 1990s have brought about the development of portable mediums with large data storage capacity as well as advancing the network infrastructures to allow for greater speed in data transmission (i.e., cable modems and digital subscriber lines) (Luckenbill and Miller, 1998; Hinduja, 2001). All of these technological advances have not only made the accessing of information easier but have also made it easier to copy and distribute copyrighted materials such as computer software, motion pictures, and music.

Piracy is the unauthorized copying of copyright material for commercial purposes and the unauthorized commercial dealing in copied materials (WIPO, 2001, p. 51). The advancements made in technology have made piracy not only much easier to accomplish, but also provide the tools at little or minimal costs and almost no risk. As the price of personal computers drop, so too do the costs associated with piracy since most of the equipment needed to engage in piracy (e.g., CD recording devices or "burners") is readily available with most personal computers. Since most households contain personal computers and dedicated internet connections, the ease of copying and distributing pirated materials can be accomplished in the ease of one's own home with little risk of detection (Hinduja, 2001). Due to the simplicity and inexpensive nature of copying materials, some have argued that piracy (particularly software piracy) is extremely widespread (Christensen and Eining, 1991).

Certain environments such as universities, governmental agencies, and businesses are conducive or supportive of piracy (primarily software piracy). In fact, the levels of piracy have become so widespread in these environments that some have argued that the behavior has become socially acceptable (Christensen and Eining, 1991). Environments, such as university settings, are actually considered to be breeding grounds for certain types of piracy (primarily software piracy) because of the heavy reliance upon computers in the environment (Sims, Cheng, and Teegen, 1996; Hinduja, 2001) and the ready and sometimes required access and use of computers to perform functions (for administrators, faculty, staff, and students alike).

Demographic or Personal Attribute Factors

Early research on the causes of intellectual property violations focused on identifying demographic and personal attribute correlates of pirating behavior in order to develop or establish a profile of those who pirate copyrighted material. The belief was that once a profile was developed it might be possible to gain insights into those who are most likely to engage in pirating behavior. Once the pirates are identified, measures and actions can then be taken to address and stop the problem of piracy. The vast majority of this research relied on student samples (both undergraduate and graduate) and inquired about computer crimes and software piracy. Student populations, it is argued, are appropriate for study for several reasons. First, software piracy is more prevalent in academia than in business and the university setting is believed to be a breeding ground for such behavior because of the large role that computers play in the daily lives of students (Sims et al., 1996; Hinduja, 2001). Second, today's students are tomorrow's managers and the behaviors that they learn in school are likely to be carried over into the workplace (Sims et al., 1996). Similarly, parental socialization (particularly in terms of parental control) can also influence youths' risk-taking attitudes and freedom to deviate from social norms (Hagan and Kay, 1990). As such these values and lessons learned early in life are likely to remain a part of the individual's repertoire. Finally, students provide a captive audience that allows researchers to inquire about causes and correlates of behavior including criminal behaviors such as software piracy.

Gender, age, level of schooling, levels of computer usage, and personal attributes are among the most commonly examined correlates. The evidence is mixed regarding the effects of gender. Some studies suggest that gender is a significant predictor of (primarily software) pirating with males more likely to engage in piracy than females (Solomon and O'Brien, 1990; Hagan and Kay, 1990; Hollinger, 1993; Simpson, Banerjee, and Simpson, 1994; Sims et al., 1996; Seale et al., 1998). Other studies, however, find no significant differences across gender in the willingness to engage in the behavior (Sacco and Zureik, 1990; Tsalikis and Ortiz-Buonafina, 1990; Davis and Welton, 1991). The effects of age indicate that younger individuals are more likely to engage in pirating behavior than older individuals though this finding is somewhat tempered by level of schooling. Research suggests that age has an indirect effect on piracy (Solomon and O'Brien, 1990; Seale et al., 1998) indicating that younger individuals are more likely to self-report engaging in the behavior. Other studies indicate that the more years of schooling, the more likely one is to pirate software. It appears that that older (college) students are more likely to pirate than younger ones (Hollinger, 1993; Sims et al., 1996). Graduate students were found to be more likely to pirate than undergraduate students (Sims et al., 1996) though several studies were unable to find significant differences between upper division undergraduates (e.g., juniors and seniors) and graduate students (Davis and Welton, 1991; Hollinger, 1993). Not surprisingly, a positive relationship has been found between levels of computer usage and piracy with those who use computers more frequently more likely to engage in software piracy (Eining and Christensen, 1991; Sims et al., 1996). In addition, various other personal attributes of self-reported pirates have been examined. These traits include intelligence, eagerness, aggressiveness, motivation, courageousness, adventuresome, and being qualified (see Seale et al., 1998 for review). It is interesting to note that this last set of characteristics are the exact same set of traits valued by society and are sought after in a good employee (Seale et al., 1998). In this way, it seems as though software piracy can be related to more general forms of white-collar crime in that the same traits that make individuals "criminal" are the same traits that make them good at their jobs. In sum, the evidence is clearly mixed regarding the relationship between demographic and personal attributes and piracy.

Deterrence

Modern deterrence theory is indebted to the Classical School of Criminology (Beccaria, 1963; Bentham, 1967) and assumes that humans are guided by reason, have free will, and are responsible for their own actions. Deterrence theory, therefore, assumes that individuals are deterred or dissuaded from criminal activities if they perceive legal sanctions to be certain, swift, and severe. The certainty of punishment refers to the probability of apprehension and being sanctioned; the swiftness of punishment refers to how quickly sanctions are imposed after the commission of the act; and severity refers to the notion that the punishment should be severe enough to outweigh the benefits gained by the commission of the crime. Hence, the deterrence approach presumes a causal effect of sanctions or the threat of imposing such sanctions (Reiss, 1984). Such a presumption assumes that the power of sanctioning violators will prohibit future violations. This presumed deterrent effect is hypothesized to operate in two ways: specific and general deterrence. The deterrence doctrine assumes that offenders who have been apprehended and punished will cease offending provided that their punishments are perceived to be severe enough (e.g., specific deterrence) and/or that those severely punished will serve as an example for the general public to instill enough fear of punishment that they will not engage in criminal behavior (e.g., general deterrence).

As originally formulated, deterrence dealt strictly with the fear of the law and legal sanctions, a notion which is commonly referred to as "mere deterrence" (Gibbs, 1975). Researchers expanded the concept of deterrence beyond the strict legal concept of formal sanctions to include "informal deterrence" or the actual or anticipated social sanctions and other consequences of crime that prevent their occurrence or reoccurrence (Akers, 2000, p. 22). Informal sanctions may include external factors such as the perception of family members, friends, and business associates who may disapprove of the act, and internal factors such as one's own conscience and moral beliefs. Informal sanctions operate in the same manner as formal sanctions in that individuals will not engage in the prospective act for fear of the informal punishment that would ensue.

Therefore, in order for formal deterrence to work there must first be a law prohibiting the behavior. In terms of intellectual property rights, there are both criminal and civil statutes designed to prevent the theft of intellectual property (see Maher and Thompson, 2002 for an overview). Deterrence assumes that people are not only aware of the laws that prohibit the behavior but are also fearful of the sanctions (both formal and informal) that may ensue. Christensen and Eining (1991) and Reid, Thompson, and Logsdon (1992) examined the impact of student knowledge of copyright laws and found that students tend to be relatively uninformed about the laws pertaining to software copyrights. Other research suggests that even when individuals are aware of the copyright laws that knowledge does little to deter the behavior. Swinyard, Rinne, and Keng (1990) found that some individuals were more influenced by the benefits of their actions than with the legal costs of their actions. Maher and Thomspson (2002) report that civil sanctions are also insufficient at deterring the theft of intellectual property rights. The lack of deterrence in this case is not because the individuals do not know the law exists but precisely the opposite: the punitive damages that result from the illegal act are simply viewed as a "cost of doing business" (Maher and Thomspon, 2002, p. 765).

The effects of informal sanctions do not fare much better in explaining theft of intellectual property rights. Seale and his colleagues (1998) found no relationship between university software policies and the reported piracy practices of university employees. Taylor and Shim (1993) also found no effect. Harrington (1989) found that situational factors such as a low likelihood of being caught and punished, behavior referent to others, and a perceived lack of clear standards of conduct were better predictors of software copying among a sample of students than were individual factors (e.g., age, socioeconomic status, and level of education). In sum, the extant research on the deterrent effects of intellectual property theft seem to show little effect. Hollinger and Lanza-Kaduce (1988) suggest that computer laws seem to serve more as a symbolic function rather than as a deterrent. The same general conclusion could be made for all of intellectual property laws.

Equity Theory

Closely related to the deterrence perspective, is the notion of equity theory (Adams, 1963). Equity theory, like deterrence, is a perceptual theory that assumes individuals are rational beings and calculate the costs and benefits of an act before choosing a course of action. The underlying impetus for equity theory is that individuals search for fairness or equity in social exchanges with the desire to maximize one's own personal outcomes. Social exchanges can include goods and services as well as conditions that affect an individual's well-being such as psychological and emotional aspects (Glass and Wood, 1996). Individuals are assumed to engage in acts as long as they perceive an equitable relationship: "An equitable relationship exists when the individual perceives that the participants in the exchange are receiving equal relative outcomes from the relationship" (Glass and Wood, 1996, p. 1191).

Reciprocation is one major class of social exchange that exists when there is a direct exchange between two parties (Eckhoff, 1974; Glass and Wood, 1996). The pirating of copyrighted goods falls within this category. For example, two friends, Heather and Jennifer, each want the most recent CD from their two favorite artists, No Doubt's *The Singles 1992-2003* and Train's *My Private Nation*, but neither girl has enough money to buy more than one CD. So, the girls decide that Heather will buy the No Doubt CD while Jennifer will buy the Train CD and then will exchange the CDs in order for each to make a copy of the other. In this instance, from the perspective of each girl, an equitable exchange has occurred. Each individual will allow the other to illegally copy the CD she purchased because they each anticipate the outcomes will outweigh or be equal to the inputs they bring to the exchange (Glass and Wood, 1996). In other words, each girl feels as though the exchange is fair and equitable and she is getting out of the exchange what she put into it, a copy of a latest CD.

While equity theory offers little explanation in terms of why one begins offending in the first place, it does offer an explanation as to why the illegal behavior continues and why it ceases. Piracy and illegal swapping of copyrighted materials is likely to continue as long as the situation and exchange is perceived by all parties to be fair and equitable. As long as the exchange is viewed by all parties to be fair and equitable, meaning that each side of the exchange feels like they are maximizing their own benefits, the more likely the motivation will remain to continue the behavior. On the other hand, as soon as one party feels that there is inequity in the exchange the behavior is likely to cease. Inequity in the exchange causes individuals to become distressed and in order to end the distress the individual is motivated to reduce the inequity of the situation (Glass and Wood, 1996).

There are two possible avenues to restore the equity in the relationship. The first enables the cessation of the criminal activity all together while the second calls for adjustment to the perceived value of the goods to be exchanged. One way to acquire equity is to restore "actual equity" by altering inputs or outcomes of the exchange (Glass and Wood, 1996). In other words, the individual can altogether remove himself from the exchange or he can alter how much he puts into the exchange. The second way is by restoring psychological equity in which the individual changes his perceptions of the value of his inputs or outcomes (Glass and Wood, 1996). In this second situation, the actual good or product being exchanged does not get altered but instead the perceived value of the object is changed.

Research has examined equity theory by focusing on the cost of the product to be copied. Parker (1976) and Harrington (1989) both find that the higher the costs of the software, the more likely it is to be copied. In terms of equity theory, individuals were more likely to engage in the behavior when they believed the results would come out in their favor. In other words, the high price of the desired outcome (i.e., the copied product) maximized their outcomes. Glass and Wood (1996) examined equity theory from a slightly different angle. They used a sample of undergraduate business students to examine how much an individual is willing to put into the exchange. By using a scenario design, Glass and Wood (1996) asked respondents how likely it would be that they would allow a fellow classmate to copy software that they had purchased for a class at varying dollar amounts ($10, $75, and $100). Consistent with equity theory, they found that the higher the cost of the software, the lower the subject's intention to allow another to copy it. Glass and Wood (1996) also included other positive and negative situational factors into the questionnaire and found that in the instances of the positive situational factors (i.e., positive social outcome or fulfilling debt requirement), the subjects were inclined to allow the software to be copied whereas with the negative situational variable (i.e., being caught in the act), the subjects were not likely to permit the copying of the software.

Ethical Decision-making Process

The premise behind the ethical decision making process is that ethics or morals influence the decision an individual will ultimately make. Those individuals who have and adhere to a high moral standard are believed to be less likely to engage in unethical behavior while those with low morals are believed to be more likely to engage in unethical behaviors. Ethical behavior refers to actions that would be both legal and morally acceptable to the larger community (Glass and Wood, 1996). Engaging in any type of criminal activity including piracy could be considered an unethical decision. This decision making model is predicated on the assumption that a person can recognize and distinguish unethical behavior. If a person is unable or unwilling to recognize the moral issue at hand, he/she will fail to use his/her morals or ethics in the decision-making process (Jones, 1991).

A substantial amount of evidence indicates that individuals do not perceive piracy to be an ethical problem. Among a sample of college students, Cohen and Cornwell (1989) found that software piracy was viewed as both acceptable and normal. Solomon and O'Brien (1990) indicate that most of their sample of college students had pirated or allowed a friend to pirate software. These same students indicated that they viewed the pirating behavior to be socially and ethically acceptable. Shim and Taylor (1989) report that in a sample of faculty members most believe that their colleagues were engaging in software piracy but did not support the pirating of software for teaching purposes.

Some research has suggested that the relationship between gender and willingness to engage in unethical behavior, such as piracy, is not well understood (Gilligan, 1982; Oz, 1990). Gilligan (1982, p. 19), for example, argues that the developmental processes of men and women differ such that female moral development focuses on the understanding of responsibility and relationships whereas male moral development centers around fairness and the understanding of rights and rules. These differences lead to distinctive ways of interpreting experiences and choices that ultimately lead to different paths for resolution. For example, males may view actors in a dilemma as opponents, whereas females will view those same actors as members of a social network upon which they all depend (Gilligan, 1982: 30). Therefore, males will tend to rely on logic and rules to dictate the path to resolution while females tend to rely on communication and care for resolution. The evidence to date is mixed regarding the differences between men and women on unethical behavior in general and pirating behavior in particular (Sims et al., 1996).

Cultural differences may also influence the ethical decision making process in that ethics and morality judgments may differ by culture or national origins. Swinyard and colleagues (1990) conducted a cross-cultural study between Singapore and the U.S in order to examine differences in morality and software piracy. Using student samples in both countries, they found that Singaporean subjects were more familiar with copyright laws but were less supportive of the laws and more likely to engage in software piracy than the American subjects. In order to explain this difference, the authors provide an explanation that focuses on cultural differences in moral decision-making. They suggest that Americans tend to be rule-oriented when it comes to making decisions while Asians lean more toward being circumstance-oriented. It appears as though Americans tend to have fundamental values of right and wrong and apply those standards to all situations. Asians, on the other hand, tend to focus more on the totality of the circumstances when making decisions.

Theory of Reasoned Action

The central feature of the theory of reasoned action is that an individual's intention to perform a given behavior is a function of the sum of their motivational influences (Ajzen and Fishbein, 1980). The main premise, then, is that a person's intention to engage in some action is the main predictor and influencer of attitude. To the extent that a person intends to do something, they will more than likely do it. But if they do not intend to do something, then they will more than likely not do it. Two main determinants of an individual's behavior under this theory are: 1) personal, or attitudinal factors, defined as the favorable (or unfavorable) evaluation of behavior, as a function of an individual's salient beliefs (i.e., suggesting that people think about their decisions and possible outcomes before making their decision), and 2) social or normative factors which includes a person's perception of what important referent groups think s/he should do (i.e., asking others their opinion before engaging in the act). At the point of decision or when confronted with a moral situation in which a choice is to be made, the theory of reasoned action argues that individuals will decide on the basis of their attitudes toward the behavior and their perceptions of what others think is appropriate.

Recently, Ajzen (1991) extended his formation of the theory of reasoned action because this earlier theory was limited in dealing with behaviors over which people had incomplete volitional control. Termed a theory of planned behavior, Ajzen argues that intentions to perform behaviors of different kinds can be predicted with high accuracy from attitudes toward the behavior, subjective norms, and perceived behavioral control. Common to both models, however, is the key assumption that "intentions are assumed to capture the motivational factors that influence a behavior; they are indications of how hard people are willing to try, of how much of an effort they are planning to exert, in order to perform the behavior" (Ajzen, 1991, p. 181).

Much research examining the theory of reasoned action has relied on scenario or vignette research designs in which the respondent is presented with a scenario, or hypothetical story in which a character portrayed in the story engages in a particular act, and asked if they would respond as the actor in the scenario did. This method has been used to examine a variety of criminal behaviors including tax evasion (Nagin and Klepper, 1989), drunk driving and shoplifting (Nagin and Paternoster, 1993; Piquero and Tibbetts, 1996) as well as corporate offending decisions (Simpson and Piquero, 2002). Research has recently applied the theory to account for software piracy, though instead of examining intentions to offend they rely on self-reported measures of piracy. Seale and his colleagues (1998) surveyed employees at a large southwestern university in order to determine if two separate factors, attitudinal and normative, existed.

They were unable to identify the two separate factors as predicted by the theory. However, they did find several factors that affected an individual's social or normative beliefs. Specifically, they found that perceived behavioral control as measured by expertise required had a direct effect on self- reported piracy. Christensen and Eining (1991) used a sample of business students in order to examine the influence of subjective or social norms (e.g., influence of organization including schools and companies and influence of friends) on self-reported piracy behavior and found a significant and positive relationship. This suggests that when an individual believes that friends and social organizations (i.e., school and place of employment) favorably view software piracy, they are more likely to report engaging in the behavior.

Learning Theory

At its core, Sutherland's (1947) theory of differential association argues that criminal behavior is learned much like non-criminal behavior is learned, through interaction with other persons in a process of communication. According to differential association, a person becomes delinquent because of an excess of definitions favorable to violation of law over definitions unfavorable to law violation. These definitions have been the source of much debate in criminology but generally involve both attitudes and behaviors. When attitudes and behaviors are more prone to crime than non-crime, the chances of criminal activity increase.

Building off the pioneering work of Sutherland regarding his differential association theory, Burgess and Akers (1966) and later Akers (1985), specified a social learning theory of criminal activity that makes use of the central concepts and principles of behaviorism. Like differential association, social learning theory maintains that criminal behavior is learned, but the way its learned is through direct operant conditioning and imitation or modeling of others. According to Akers, behavior is learned or conditioned as a result of the effects (outcomes, consequences) it has on an individual (i.e., instrumental conditioning). There are two major processes involved in instrumental conditioning, reinforcement and punishment, and each of these may take two forms negative and positive. Reinforcement causes a behavior to increase in frequency. This can occur through positive reinforcement (rewarding of behavior) or negative reinforcement (if engaging in a behavior allows a person to prevent an unpleasant stimulus). Punishment can be positive (e.g., when an unpleasant response follows a behavior) or negative (e.g., if a reward is removed in response to a behavior). According to Akers, Krohn, Lanza-Kaduce, and Radosevich (1979, p. 638), "whether deviant or conforming behavior is acquired and persists depends on past and present rewards or punishments for the behavior and the rewards and punishments attached to alternative behavior." Recently, Akers (1998) further extended his individual social learning theory to include the influence of the social structure (SSSL). The basic assumption behind SSSL is that social learning is the primary process linking social structure to individual behavior. The main proposition of SSSL is that variations in the social structure, culture, and locations of individuals and groups in the social system explain variation in crime rates, principally through their information on differences among individuals on the key social learning theory variables (Akers, 1998, p. 322). In sum, social learning theories of criminality contend that individuals learn to engage in crime primarily through their associations with others and in particular through the constellation of rewards and punishments.

More often than not the primary variable that is used in testing social learning theory is the behavior of peer groups. Several studies of software piracy also rely on this variable to examine the influence of peers on an individual's self-reported pirating behavior. For example, using a sample of college students, Hollinger (1993) examined two types of computer crime, giving or receiving pirated computer software and accessing another's computer account or files without the owner's knowledge or permission. He found that friends' involvement in piracy was strongly correlated with self-reported computer crime. More specifically, only 2 percent of the sample was likely to engage in computer crime when they reported that their best friends were not likely to engage in computer crime. However, almost 40 percent of the sample admitted to engaging in computer crime when they reported that more than half of their best friends engage in the same behavior.

Skinner and Fream (1997) conduct a direct test of social learning theory using a sample of undergraduate students who reported their involvement in five types of computer crime: software piracy, guessing a password to gain unauthorized access, gaining unauthorized access for the purpose of browsing, gaining unauthorized access for the purpose of changing information, and wrote or used a program that would destroy someone's computerized data (i.e., creating a computer virus). They found that associating with peers who participate in computer crime was the strongest predictor of their computer crime index (which was created by summing the frequency measure that asked students how often in the past year they committed each of the five computer crimes). In addition, they found that the source of imitation is learned not only from peer groups, but from a variety of sources including parents, siblings, teachers, and virtual peer groups or computer bulletin boards where interaction occurs electronically.

Prevention of Intellectual Property Theft

One of the primary reasons we attempt to understand the causes and correlates of criminal behavior is so that we are able to develop intervention and prevention efforts designed to control the behavior. Strategies to control behavior can be regarded as either primarily focusing on preventive behaviors (front-end strategies) or as deterrents (back-door strategies), and even further some strategies do not simply attempt to make the offense "harder" or less rewarding, but to reduce or eliminate opportunity. Preventive controls are designed to make criminal activities harder or less rewarding for perpetrators by increasing the costs of engaging in the criminal act (Gopal and Sanders, 1997). Deterrent controls, on the other hand, intend to avoid criminal activities altogether by dissuading the users from even considering engaging in the act (Gopal and Sanders, 1997). A variety of different prevention techniques have been employed in order to prevent the theft of intellectual property rights but these efforts have primarily been designed on an ad hoc basis.

One of the most common prevention strategies employed is to use technological advances to increase the costs of engaging in piracy. These antipiracy technologies include strategies such as using encryption technology to make it harder for pirates to intercept the information while it is being transmitted, the use of special codes that would only allow access to the authorized owner, offering customer support to only the legal owner, and using hardware locks. Each technological advancement is designed to try and stay one step ahead of the pirates in order to dissuade them from engaging in piracy. The problem with this type of strategy is that some may find the challenge of breaking the new protective barrier as a rewarding experience rather than a hindrance to pirating (Sims et al., 1996).

Another approach that also utilizes technological advancements is to use the technology to give the public what it wants. In other words, rather than trying to fight the use of new advances in technology some companies are finding ways to use the technology in their favor. For example, the prolific Internet source, Napster, drew much attention for the illegal downloading and sharing of copyrighted music. Napster provided a peer-to-peer file sharing service that allowed individuals to post and download music through the transmission of MP3 music files without legally purchasing the songs. Record companies along with artists fought hard and won the battle to shut down the illegal Napster service but recognized the potential of peer-to-peer file sharing services (*A&M et al. v. Napster*; *Metallica v. Napster*). New legal music services are now available that allow individuals to download their favorite music for either a one-time download fee (e.g., iTunes) or as a monthly service (e.g., Napster).

Since many students reported not knowing intellectual property laws (see Christensen and Eining, 1991), roughly 50 percent had indicated they had read the licensing agreement that appears on most copyrighted software programs, another deterrent strategy, educating the public, may be warranted. (Note: Still, it remains unknown if 100 percent read these agreements—that is, were knowledgeable about the legal rights of copyright holders—patterns of behavior would change.) One such method that is being used is a public educational campaign. The MPAA continues to engage in this effort in order to teach the public that movie piracy is illegal, to explain how it impacts the economy and impacts the jobs of many people who work in the motion picture industry. The current phase of the educational program is designed to target daily newspapers, consumer magazines, college newspapers, as well as anti-piracy messages appearing in local theaters to help inform the public about the negative consequences of pirating behavior. Other industries, such as the software industry, maintain anti-piracy speaker bureaus and distribute informational videos to their consumers how their goods should and should not be used (Luckenbill and Miller, 1998). Finally, educators are also advocating for the inclusion of ethical components into courses in order to educate students about the proper uses of intellectual property (Simpson et al., 1994).

Industries have also created or hired units, such as trade associations, to look after and protect their property. For example, the MPAA has it's own security office to aid in the fight against film piracy (Luckenbill and Miller, 1998). The duties of the MPAA security office include setting up hotlines that allow them to receive tips or reports of pirating behavior, tracking the process of cases as they move through our legal system, and keeping records (Luckenbill and Miller, 1998). In addition to these private policing responsibilities, trade associations also allow the industry to have a collective voice and more resources to help mobilize legal resources against the pirating behavior. Trade associations can lobby for the interest of the industry as a whole and in some instances have proven to be quite successful. For example, the U.S. Senate Bill 893 (effective October 28, 1992) was created as a response to the pressure of the software industry and increased the penalties for copyright infringement (Cheng, Sims, and Teegen, 1997, p. 50).

The last strategy used to try and control the theft of intellectual property is by means of lawsuits (both civil and criminal) and legal statutes in order to deter pirating behavior. Enlisting the help of the government by means of legislative action is an avenue that is being aggressively pursued. Many trade associations have not only fought to get laws passed that prohibit the theft of intellectual property rights but have also filed their own lawsuits against individuals. Many criminal statutes against theft of intellectual property are currently on the books with many of the laws specific to certain forms of intellectual property. For example, the Economic Espionage Act of 1996 makes the theft of trade secrets a federal crime while the Trademark Counterfeiting Act of 1984 criminalizes the trafficking of counterfeit goods and services (Maher and Thompson, 2002).

Unfortunately, while each of these strategies in isolation has been well documented and implemented in a number of arenas, there have been no outcome evaluation efforts that have examined the effectiveness of each of the interventions. In addition, we know almost nothing about the changes in intellectual property violations (both by amount and type) that have occurred in response to these prevention and intervention efforts. This is unfortunate since many of these efforts are costly in terms of both time and financial resources that are needed for proper implementation. A clear understanding of the impact of these efforts on intellectual property violations is imperative to help guide public policies designed to combat piracy and protect the rights of intellectual property owners.

Agenda for Future Research

As has been made clear, the current state of knowledge regarding the nature and prevalence of intellectual property theft is scant. A three-pronged research effort is suggested that may be ambitious— but always relevant in helping to begin to fill some of the gaps that remain in the knowledge base regarding the theft of intellectual property rights. These three priorities surround data collection efforts, theoretical tests, and cataloging and evaluating the knowledge base regarding the effects of policy efforts.

First, just as the U.S. Bureau of Census together with the Bureau of Justice Statistics conducts a nationwide survey of crime victims, efforts must be developed to initiate a nationwide data collection effort that targets information regarding the prevalence of intellectual property theft with special attention made to include all varieties of intellectual property violations (i.e., copyright, patents, trademarks, and trade secrets). This data collection effort need not be separate from those that are currently conducted but new questions will obviously need to be added. This nationwide data collection would also benefit from asking respondents about their knowledge of laws pertaining to and regarding intellectual property rights (e.g., copyright laws). It would be useful to understand whether persons are knowledgeable about such laws in an effort to aid public policy responses for intervention and prevention efforts. Although there are industry specific measures available on trends regarding violations of intellectual property rights (e.g., copyright violations including music piracy), this data has been gathered by those agencies and organizations that have a vested interest in the outcome (e.g., RIAA) so an independent source of information would help to aid in the understanding of the nature and prevalence of this kind of theft here in the U.S. Ideally, international victimization data would also be collected as well in order to understand the global impact of these types of offenses.

Second, currently there is very little information known about the causes and correlates of intellectual property theft and what little information is known seems to raise more questions than it answers. For example, do the theoretical explanations offered earlier predict all types of intellectual property theft equally well or does theft of intellectual property fall better under the purview of one theory (i.e., social learning) than another (i.e., ethics)? Or is an integration of various frameworks best suited for the understanding of this type of behavior? Some of the theories already outlined seek to explain the onset of this kind of behavior while others focus on explaining persistence and desistence of intellectual property right violations. Ideally we would want to understand why individuals start offending, what causes them to continue, and why they stop. In addition, very little is known about the differences at the individual (i.e., micro) and group (i.e., macro) level. Are some theories better equipped to understand intellectual property violations at the micro-level while others better inform us of offending at the macro-level? While some research has suggested that piracy is more prevalent among younger individuals (i.e., college students) we know nothing regarding this type of crime over an individual's life course (though Oz (1990) suggests that the offending behavior is established long before the individual enters the workforce). Therefore, are some theories more relevant to an earlier phase as opposed to later part of an individual's life-course? Other issues regarding the opportunity to offend also arise. Do the correlates of intellectual property violations (as well as the various types) differ across samples (i.e., general population, business executives and managers, high school students, college students) both domestically and abroad? Similarly, how are the opportunities to offend distributed across different populations? Some evidence seems to suggest that those who use the computer more often are more likely to report engaging in software piracy (Eining and Christensen, 1991; Sims et al., 1996) but as of yet no study has directly examined the influence of exposure time and access to the computer or access to internet services on pirating behavior. In short, a series of small-scale well-designed surveys could provide important baseline information regarding the causes of intellectual property theft.

Third, policy options, responses, intervention, and prevention efforts aimed at curtailing intellectual property violations seem to be changing almost daily. It would be useful for researchers to catalog these efforts and explain their changing manifestations over time. For example, many of the prevention efforts that have been put into place are industry specific. The efforts put into place that surround music piracy, such as only allowing a song to be copied a certain number of times, may and often times do differ from the efforts aimed at deterring individuals from copying the latest movies. Many of these efforts have considered and implemented technological advancements that make it more difficult to copy products. In that regard, it would be interesting to understand individual's responses to these efforts and if they have become deterred or more determined to engage (or continue) the behavior.

Copyright laws and enforcement of their violations have been ill-studied in the social sciences. While legal studies have kept track of and documented the ever-changing laws and legal statutes regarding the theft of intellectual property rights (see Maher and Thomspon, 2002 for review), very little is known on how these laws impact the public at large and more specifically the effects the laws have on the offending behavior. For example, record shows that were prevalent during the 1980s where it was common to buy bootlegged records and concerts have pretty much ceased to exist. It is unclear if these outlets were shut down due to the changes in laws protecting copyrighted works, such as the bootlegged music being sold, or if the sales of such illegal goods simply was displaced to other venues (many are found on Ebay). Recent news reports have indicated that local area flea markets have become targeted locations cracking down on the illegal sales of copyrighted CDs and DVDs. Such interventions require the cooperation of local and federal law enforcement as well as the cooperation of the recording and/or the motion picture associations. Understanding not only the costs and consequences of such actions but the larger impact on society is only one piece to the overall puzzle regarding the full range of available responses to the theft of intellectual property rights.

In short, although the legal arena has been witness to much research on the theft of intellectual property rights, the same cannot be said from the social scientific community generally, and the criminological community in particular. This is a bit surprising since criminology contains the theories and requisite methodological tools needed to effectively understand and document the problem of intellectual property theft. The Department of Justice and its research arm, the National Institute of Justice, stands in a good position to begin local and nationwide efforts together in an effort to document the nature and prevalence of intellectual property rights violations as well as cataloging and evaluating policy efforts already put into place. It is important that such research-based efforts are stepped up and executed quickly so that the needed data can be collected and used to help inform the public policy issues, discussions, and decisions that surround the theft of intellectual property rights. Nowhere and at no time has this been as important of an issue as it is in today's digital age. If America wants to continue to be a world leader in the production of intellectual property, a more complete understanding of the prevalence and causes of the problem are needed as well as avenues which can help prevent the theft from occurring.

References

Adams, J.S. (1963). Toward an understanding of inequity. *Journal of Abnormal and Social Psychology, 67*, 422-436.

Ajzen, I. (1991). The theory of planned behavior. *Organizational Behavior and Human Decision Processes, 50*, 179-211.

Ajzen, I., and Fishbein, M. (1980). *Understanding Attitudes and Predicting Social Behaviour.* Englewood Cliffs, NJ: Prentice Hall.

Akers, R.L. (1985). *Deviant Behavior: A Social Learning Approach* (3rd ed.). Belmont, CA: Wadsworth.

Akers, R.L. (1998). *Social Learning and Social Structure: A General Theory of Crime and Deviance.* Boston, MA: Northeastern University Press.

Akers, R.L. (2000). *Criminological Theories: Introduction, Evaluation, and Application* (3rd ed.). Los Angeles, CA: Roxbury Publishing Company.

Akers, R.L., Krohn, M.D., Lanza-Kaduce, L., and Radosevich, M. (1979). Social learning and deviant behavior: A specific test of a general theory. *American Sociological Review, 44*, 635-655.

Beccaria, C. (1963). *On Crimes and Punishment.* New York: MacMillan Publishing.

Bentham, J. (1967). *A Fragment on Government and an Introduction to the Principal of Morals and Legislation.* Oxford: Basil Blackwell.

Burgess, R.L., and Akers, R.L. (1966). A different association-reinforcement theory of criminal behavior. *Social Problems, 14*, 128-147.

Carruthers, B.G., and Ariovich, L. (2004). The sociology of property rights. *Annual Review of Sociology, 30*, 23-46.

Cheng, H. K., Sims, R.R., and Teegen, H. (1997). To purchase or to pirate software: An empirical study. *Journal of Management Information Systems, 13*, 49-60.

Christensen, A.L., and Eining, M. M. (1991). Factors influencing software piracy: Implication for accountants. *Journal of Information Systems, Spring*, 67-80.

Cohen, L.E., and Felson, M. (1979). Social change and crime rate trends: A routine activities approach. *American Sociological Review, 44*, 588-608.

Cohen, E., and Cornwell, L. (1989). A question of ethics: Developing information systems ethics. *Journal of Business Ethics, 8*, 431-437.

Davis, J. R., and Welton, R. E. (1991). Professional ethics: Business students perceptions.' *Journal of Business Ethics, 10*, 451-463.

Dusollier, S. (2003). Open source and copyleft: Authorship reconsidered? *Columbia Journal of Law and the Arts, 26*, 281-296.

Eckhoff, T. (1974). *Justice: Its Determinants in Social Interaction.* Rotterdam, Netherlands: Rotterdam University Press.

Eining, M.M., and Christensen, A.L. (1991). A psycho-social model of software piracy: The development and test of a model. In R.M. Dejoie, G.C. Fowler, and D.B. Paradice (Eds.), *Ethical Issues in Information Systems* (pp. 182-188). Boston, MA: Boyd and Fraser.

Endeshaw, A. (2002). The paradox of intellectual property lawmaking in the new millennium: Universal templates as terms of surrender for the non-industrial nations; piracy as an offshoot. *Cardozo Journal of International and Comparative Law, 10*, 47-77.

Gasaway, L.N. (2003). America's cultural record: A thing of the past? *Houston Law Review, 40*, 643-671.

Gibbs, J. (1975). *Crime, Punishment, and Deterrence.* New York: Elsevier.

Gilligan, C. (1982). *In a Different Voice: Psychological Theory and Women's Development.* Cambridge, MA: Harvard University Press.

Glass, R.S., and Wood, W.A. (1996). Situational determinants of software piracy: An equity theory perspective. *Journal of Business Ethics, 15*, 1189-1198.

Gopal, R.D., and Sanders, G. L. (1997). Preventive and deterrent controls for software piracy. *Journal of Management Information Systems, 13*, 29-47.

Gottfredson, M., and Hirschi, T. (1990). *A General Theory of Crime.* Palo Alto, CA: Stanford University Press.

Hagan, J., and Kay, F. (1990). Gender and delinquency in white-collar families: A power-control perspective. *Crime and Delinquency, 36*, 391-407.

Harrington, S. (1989). Why people copy software and create computer viruses: Individual characteristics or situational factors. *Information Resource Management Journal*, 28-37.

Hinduja, S. (2001). Correlates of internet software piracy. *Journal of Contemporary Criminal Justice, 17*, 369-382.

Hollinger, R.C. (1993). Crime by computer: Correlates of software piracy and unauthorized account access. *Security Journal, 2*, 2-12.

Hollinger, R.C., and Lanza-Kaduce, L. (1988). The process of criminalization: The case of computer crime laws. *Criminology, 26*, 101-126.

IFPI. (2003). *The record industry commercial piracy report, 2003.* London: IFPI.

Jones, T.M. (1991). Ethical decision making by individuals in organizations: An issue-contingent model. *Academy of Management Review, 16*, 366-395.

Lessig, L. (2001). *The Future of Ideas: The Fate of the Commons in a Connected World.* New York: Random House.

Luckenbill, D.F., and Miller, S.L. (1998). Defending intellectual property: State efforts to protect creative works. *Justice Quarterly, 15*, 93-120.

Maher, M.K., and Thomson, J.M. (2002). Intellectual property crimes. *American Criminal Law Review, 39*, 763-816.

Moohr, G.S. (2003). The crime of copyright infringement: An inquiry based on morality, harm, and criminal theory. *Boston University Law Review, 83*, 731-783.

MPA. (2003). *2003 Piracy Fact Sheets: US Overview.* MPA Worldwide Market Research.

Nagin, D., and Klepper, S. (1989). Tax compliance and perceptions of the risks of detection and criminal prosecution. *Law and Society Review, 23*, 209-240.

Nagin, D., and Paternoster, R. (1993). Enduring individual differences and rational choice theories of crime. *Law and Society Review, 27*, 467-496.

Oz, E. (1990). The attitude of managers-to-be toward software piracy. *OR/MS Today, August*, 24-26.

Parker, D.B. (1976). *Crime by Computer.* New York: Charles Scribner and Sons.

Patry, W. (2003). The United States and international copyright law: From Berne to Eldred. *Houston Law Review, 40*, 749-762.

Piquero, A., and Tibbetts, S. (1996). Specifying the direct and indirect effects of low self-control and situational factors in offenders' decision making: Toward a more complete model of rational offending. *Justice Quarterly, 13*, 481-510.

Poltorak, A.I., and Lerner, P.J. (2002). *Essentials of Intellectual Property.* New York: John Wiley and Sons, Inc.

Reid, R.A., Thompson, J.K., and Logsdon, J.M. (1992). Knowledge and attitudes of management students toward software piracy. *Journal of Computer Information Systems, 33*, 46-51.

Reiss, Jr., A.J. (1984). Selecting strategies of social control over organizational life. In K. Hawkins and J.M. Thomas (Eds.), *Enforcing Regulation* (pp. 23-35). Boston, MA: Kluwer-Nijoff Publishing.

Ronkainen, I.A., and Guerrero-Cusumano, J. (2001). Correlates of intellectual property violations. *Multinational Business Review, 9*, 59-65.

Sacco, V.F., and Zureik, E. (1990). Correlates of computer misuse: Data from a self-reporting sample. *Behaviour and Information Technology, 9*, 353-369.

Seale, D.A., Polakowski, M., and Schneider, S. (1998). It's not really theft!: Personal and workplace ethics that enable software piracy. *Behaviour and Information Technology, 17*, 27-40.

Shim, J.P., and Taylor, G.S. (1989). Practicing manager's perception/attitude toward illegal software copying. *OR/MS Today, 16*, 30-33.

Simpson, S.S., and Piquero, N.L. (2002). Low self control, organizational offending and corporate crime. *Law and Society Review, 36*, 509-547.

Simpson, P.M., Banerjee, D., and Simpson, Jr., C.L. (1994). Softlifting: A model of motivating factors. *Journal of Business Ethics, 13*, 431-438.

Sims, R.R., Cheng, H.K., and Teegen, H. (1996). Toward a profile of student software pirates. *Journal of Business Ethics, 15*, 839-849.

Skinner, W., and Fream, A.M. (1997). A social learning analysis of computer crime among college students. *Journal of Research in Crime and Delinquency, 34*, 495-522.

Solomon, S.L., and O'Brien, J.A. (1990). The effect of demographic factors on attitudes toward software piracy. *Journal of Information Systems, 30*, 40-46.

Stim, R. (2000). *Intellectual property: Patents, trademarks, and copyrights* (2nd ed.). Albany, NY: West Thomas Learning.

Story, A. (2003). Burn Berne: Why the leading international copyright convention must be repealed. *Houston Law Review, 40*, 763-801.

Sutherland, E. (1947). *Principles of Criminology*. Philadelphia, PA: Lippincott.

Swinyard, W.R., Rinne, H., and Keng Kau, A. (1990). The morality of software piracy: A cross-cultural analysis. *Journal of Business Ethics, 9*, 655-664.

Taylor, G.S., and Shim, J.P. (1993). A comparative examination of attitudes toward software piracy among business professors and executives. *Human Relations, 46*, 419-433.

Thong, J.Y.L., and Yap, C. (1998). Testing an ethical decision-making theory: The case of softlifting. *Journal of Management Information Systems, 15*, 213-237.

Tsalikis, J., and Ortiz-Buonafina, M. (1990). Ethical beliefs' differences of males and females. *Journal of Business Ethics, 9*, 509-517.

USTR. (2004). *2003 Special 301 Report*. Washington, DC: Office of the US Trade Representative.

Volokh, E. (2003). Freedom of speech and intellectual property: Some thoughts after Eldred, 44 Liquormart, and Bartnicki. *Houston Law Review, 40*, 697-748.

Yen, A.C. (2003). Eldred, the first amendment, and aggressive copyright claims. *Houston Law Review, 40*, 673-695.

WIPO (2001) *WIPO Intellectual Property Handbook: Policy, Law, and Use*. Geneva, Switzerland. WIPO Publication. No. 489(E).

Zeithaml, V. (1988). Consumer perceptions of price, quality, and value: A means-end model and synthesis of evidence. *Journal of Marketing, 52*, 2-22.

4

Intellectual Property and White-collar Crime: Report of Issues, Trends, and Problems for Future Research

Annette Beresford, Christian Desilets,
Sandy Haantz, John Kane, and April Wall
National White Collar Crime Center (NW3C)

Intellectual property (IP) can be thought of as any product of the human intellect that is deemed unique and potentially valuable in the marketplace, including an idea, invention, literary creation, unique name, business method, industrial process, chemical formula, and computer program. Since the creation and dissemination of IP is considered an important part of economic, social, and cultural development, laws have been created throughout the world to define and protect the rights of those who develop IP. These laws include protections through patents, copyrights, trademarks, and trade secrets, and are enforced primarily through civil action and criminal prosecution.

Views on the appropriate role of law in the development of IP vary tremendously among economists, political theorists, sociologists, the legal community, law enforcement, and others. Since current systems of IP law include the criminalization of IP use and exchange, examining these differing views is an important part of evaluating IP and intellectual property rights (IPR). Such a multifaceted approach to analyzing IP issues has become particularly important in recent years, as Internet and other technologies that facilitate dissemination and reproduction of information and products have become more accessible and sophisticated, and the controversies surrounding IP have become more complex. At the core of these controversies, issues of free speech and access to essential technologies are rivaled against interests in reasonable economic benefit from innovative ideas and stimulation of research and development (R&D).

Concerns about the development and application of IP law are also complicated by the fact that IPR violations are increasingly found to be associated with other crimes. For example, profits reaped from illegal sales of counterfeited goods have been associated with terrorism. Misappropriated IP has also been used to facilitate fraudulent sales, investment scams, and identity theft. In other words, violations of IP laws not only can be explicitly identified as crimes (specifically, white-collar crimes), they also can be identified as facilitators of other crimes about which there is little debate over resulting harm to the public.

In 2003-2004, the National White Collar Crime Center (NW3C) conducted a study to examine the association between IP and other white-collar crimes (WCC). The goal of this study was to identify future research that would benefit policy makers (in developing IP law); federal, state, and local agencies (in enforcing IP law); and the general public (in understanding IP issues). The study objectives were to canvass mainstream and marginal views on IP laws and to identify major problems associated with IP violations, including the facilitation of other WCC, such as investment fraud, money laundering, and identity theft. The methods for attaining these objectives included a review of literature in a variety of relevant fields, a review of information and data on IPR violations and WCC, and inquiry in areas that directly deal with IP laws and enforcement practices, such as law enforcement agencies, IP-based industries, and private litigation firms. This report outlines some of the findings of this study.

Theoretical Bases for IP Protections

By most accounts, justification for IP laws is based on the view that strict protections of IPR are the best, if not the only, means of stimulating innovation and ultimately economic growth. Despite widespread support of this view, opposition to IP protections has persisted for centuries (Kanwar and Evenson, 2001). Recent arguments favoring weak IPR protections include the contention that levels of IPR protections can be *inversely* related to innovation, economic growth, and global health. Specifically, it is argued, weak protections tend to keep market prices low, thus stimulating economic growth; and strong protections, "by creating a monopoly, may induce the producer to accumulation 'sleeping patents' in an effort to preserve market share (Kanwar and Evenson, 2001, p. 5)," thus stifling both innovation and economic growth. In addition, strong protections could, according to some, threaten global health because they reduce access to life-saving medicines, particularly in developing countries (Kamal and Bailey, 2003). Although this on-going, and currently unresolved, argument has produced more questions than solutions, in part because of the "lack of cumulative empirical evidence (Kanwar and Evenson, 2001, p. 3)," the dialogue is a useful complement to a summary of enforcement practices and problems for an assessment of future needs in IP research.

Intellectual Property from an Economic Perspective

From an economic perspective, a primary purpose of IP laws, like many other laws, is to produce a desired result that market forces fail to produce. Specifically, IP laws are designed, in part, to protect future economic gain from IP products as an incentive for investing in R&D today. Without such protections, it is assumed that innovation would decline because initial costs cannot be recovered in a free market environment (Arrow, 1962). Addressing this problem, economist Paul Romer (1990) suggested in the 1980s and 1990s that economic variables such as taxes, interest, and government subsidies could help to balance inequities that market forces fail to correct. In other words, fiscal and monetary policy could provide incentives for innovation. Other economists have argued that innovation can thrive in perfectly competitive markets and that "copyrights and patents may be socially undesirable (Boldrin and Levine, 2003, p. 1)." To support this argument, some have pointed out that the strengthening of patent protections in the 1980s "ushered in a period of stagnant, if not declining, R&D among those industries and firms that patented most (Bessen and Maskin, 2000, p. 2)." Both of these positions acknowledge that IP laws play an important role in balancing the incentives for IP production with the needs of the public.

The U.S. Supreme Court has stated that "(t)he economic philosophy behind the clause empowering Congress to grant patents and copyrights is the conviction that encouragement of individual effort by personal gain is the best way to advance public welfare through the talents of authors and inventors (*Mazer v. Stein*, 1954)." However, "(t)he primary objective of copyright [and patents] is not to reward the labor of authors [and inventors], but 'to promote the Progress of Science and useful Arts (*Feist Publications v. Rural Tel. Serv. Co.*, 1991).'" Accordingly, some have argued that any extension of IPR protections that impedes the progress of science or the arts runs counter to the Constitution. A more moderate version of this view is the belief that an author or inventor "should be rewarded up to the point at which the 'legislation will stimulate the producer' more than the monopoly rights given to the owner will harm the public ("The Criminalization," 1999, p. 1078)."

Although a number of economic models have been advanced as an alternative to the current IP system, many have been criticized as only applicable to IP industries that require small initial investments, such as the music industry. Industries that require substantial R&D funds, such as the pharmaceutical industry, may require assurances of economic return, which are not provided in these alternative models. One product of this debate is the suggestion that it may be useful to develop laws and practices that make a distinction between different types and uses of IP.

Political Theories of Intellectual Property Rights

Although justification for IP laws rely heavily on economic assumptions, they also rely on political theories, such as those that assert that ideas should be regarded as property and government should protect these forms of property. Therefore, examination of IPR should include analysis of underlying political theories to determine if the consequences of IP laws are consistent with established belief systems of the society in which the laws apply. For example, U.S. public policy is (in theory) designed to secure and promote general welfare (i.e., make people's lives better) and protect individual rights. However, IP law that is based on protections of individual rights (of control and economic benefit) without consideration of the effects of IP law on all people, or vise versa, is not consistent with the belief systems of the U.S.

Considering this conflict of interest, political theorist Robert Ostergard examined in 1999 "two dominant ... lines of reasoning (p. 157)" for the justification of IP rights: John Locke's labor theory of property and a traditional doctrine of utilitarianism. The former provides a micro perspective, focusing primarily on individual rights, and the latter provides a macro perspective, focusing primarily on group benefit. He concluded that these lines of reason, even when considered together, "do not constitute an adequate or coherent prescriptive theory for the recognition of IP rights (p. 157)."

Locke's labor theory of property contends that "objects produced by an individual through the mixing of labor with resources are the property of that individual alone (Ostergard, 1999, p. 159)." Although this dictum is centrally concerned with individual rights, it also requires that "others are not made worse off by the acquisition," which raises the question, what is "worse off"? One answer is that individuals are worse off if "they lose the opportunity to improve their situation (p. 160)." Based on this definition, Ostergard argued, "those who are monetarily restricted from buying a new drug that can save their lives are worse off (p. 162)"; therefore, IP laws—as they are currently designed—cannot be justified with Locke's labor theory. To address this problem, Ostergard suggested that a distinction be made between "essential" and "non-essential intellectual objects," using a "physical well-being criteria" to mark the difference. Others have proposed that "essential" IP should include objects that *enhance* people's well-being (Sen, 1996), such as music and cinema.

The second justification for IP rights—utilitarianism—is centrally concerned with advancing the welfare of the group (i.e., society) (Ostergard, 1999). This line of reasoning supports IP rights because they provide "an incentive for invention and production, which, ultimately promotes economic growth (p. 165)." In other words, the short-term costs of providing property rights to creators of IP are justified by the long-term benefits of promoting economic growth. Citing examples from the histories of the United States, Great Britain, China, and other countries, however, Ostergard argued that access to ideas, which is generally restricted by granting exclusive IPR, has proven to be essential in developmental stages of economic growth. Restricting access to IP, therefore, does not clearly produce long-term benefits of economic growth. This argument is particularly crucial for consideration of the impact of IP laws on developing countries in the early stages of economic growth.

An alternative conceptualization of IPR, Ostergard (1999) suggested, is one that considers "society's development at the individual level instead of at the national level (p. 168)." For example, he suggested that "whatever property is needed to maintain an individual's physical well-being must be accessible if all human beings are to be

permitted to achieve their full potential (p. 170)." In addition to attempting to accommodate both individual rights and general welfare, this
alternative attempts to address international concerns such as the safety
of counterfeit drugs that dominate the markets in many developing countries. The Nigerian Institute of Pharmaceutical Research, for example,
has determined that 80 percent of drugs in the major pharmacy stores in
Lagos, Nigeria are counterfeit ("Nigeria Reaffirms," 2003). The dangers
of this situation were demonstrated in a case involving counterfeit cough
syrup that was actually antifreeze. One hundred children died in this case.
In China, the Shenzhen Evening News reported that 192,000 people died
from the use of counterfeit drugs.

Some of the questions that both economic and political analyses raise
are: Should IP laws distinguish between different forms and uses of IP?
Should general welfare be given greater consideration than economic
benefit? Should IP laws be different for international application than
national application?

IPR Violations and Other Crimes

Based on current U.S. law, violations of IPR can be classified as a
form of white-collar crime (WCC). Broadly speaking, WCC includes
illegal activity that usually involves deceptive practices for the purpose
of financial gain. A common understanding of WCC is that it is associated with a legitimate organization or occupation and that it entails
a violation of trust. This definition extends beyond the traditional
definition of WCC as crime committed by people of high social status
(Sutherland, 1983) to include offenders from all social backgrounds
and organizations whose principal activities are criminal. Applying
this definition, IPR violations can be recognized not only as a form
of WCC in themselves, but also as a component of WCC activity that
includes multiple forms of WCC.

One of the greatest public concerns about IPR violations is the
threat to public health and safety, not only in foreign countries, but
also in the United States. For example, in Los Angeles, investigators
arrested five people in connection with the distribution of counterfeited power tools, which were marked with brand names such as
Makita, Black and Decker, and DeWalt and bore counterfeited stick-
ers to indicate that the tools had been inspected and certified as safe
(Los Angeles Police Department, 2003). In this case, more than $9.7
million in counterfeit merchandise was recovered. Other cases have

identified counterfeit vehicle and aircraft parts as posing a danger to the public (Stern, 1996), and, of course, counterfeit drugs and medical supplies (ETHICON Inc., 2003).

In addition to the concern that IPR violations are a threat to public health and safety, increasing concern has developed over the relationship between IPR violations and other crimes, including the following:

- Investment fraud (e.g., using a trademark of a legitimate company to deceive investors);
- Money laundering (e.g., concealing funds acquired from fraudulent sales);
- Fraudulent sales (e.g., creating a bogus Web site to deceive customers);
- Identity theft (e.g., using personal information acquired from a misappropriated database);
- Other online scams (e.g., fraudulently acquiring donations using the logo of a legitimate charity);
- Racketeering (e.g., organized efforts to misappropriate IP); and
- Tax evasion (e.g., failing to report income acquired through IP violations).

The Internet is one of the most easily accessible venues for the illegal use of IP as a facilitator for other criminal activity. In a case of investment fraud, for example, a Pairgain company employee used trademarks and other symbols copied from the Internet to create a Web page that appeared to be a Bloomberg financial Web page and posted a fraudulent news report about Pairgain on the site (United States Security and Exchange Commission, 1999). Because of the apparent legitimacy of the report, the employee was able to manipulate the price of Pairgain stock and make a profit by selling his personally held stock at artificially inflated prices. Since WCC is largely based on deception, and IP such as a trademark can represent a company or product that is recognized as valuable or reliable, it is not surprising that IP violations are often coupled with other WCC.

Another WCC that is frequently associated with IP violations is money laundering. The prevalence of this association prompted an amendment to the federal money laundering statute in 1988, extending the definition of "specified illegal activity (Money Laundering Control Act, § 1956)" to encompass copyright infringement. In the mid-1990s, another amendment extended the definition further to include trafficking in counterfeit goods and services. The consequence of these changes is that any use of money derived from certain types of IPR violations to fund specific forms of crime is considered money laundering, as are any attempts to disguise the origin or ownership of funds derived from illegal activity through financial transactions.

One case that has applied the rules of money laundering in an IPR violation case involved a computer salesman, Hou Wu Ding. Mr. Ding sold counterfeited computer parts and software significantly below market price at computer trade shows (Lee, 2001). In addition, authorities discovered, he hid the proceeds of these sales (more than $3.1 million) in four bank accounts by making 376 separate deposits, each below the $10,000 reporting threshold for currency transactions reports. Initially arrested on charges of money laundering and conspiracy in connection with a counterfeit software and computer parts distribution ring, Ding pled guilty to structuring currency transactions, i.e., money laundering (United States Department of Justice, 2001).

Many cases of IP violations, whether they accompany other crime or not, are never reported to law enforcement. Private companies may be reluctant to report instances of IP violations, or even file for civil remedies, because of the concern that public knowledge of such cases could damage their reputation. For example, in 2003, a Malaysian counterfeit ring penetrated the computer system of the Platte Valley Bank to steal customer debit card numbers (U.S. Bank, 2003). In this case, the debit card numbers were used to make numerous unauthorized charges against customer accounts. Instead of contacting law enforcement, the bank identified the affected debit cards and blocked the fraudulent transactions. A decision was made by the bank president to absorb the costs from damages and protect the reputation of the bank rather than undergo scrutiny by law enforcement and customers.

Controversial Applications of IP Law

A major source of conflict in the IP debate is differences in cultural norms, not only among social communities defined by geography but also among those defined by age or behavior. People who associate themselves with the Internet culture, for example, often have different beliefs about appropriate uses IP than people in the law enforcement community. Each set of beliefs is based on legal and ethical considerations, and, more importantly, has visceral meaning for community members, which is not easily relinquished.

With the significant expansion of Internet use, "dilution" has become a primary area of dispute in trademark law, and attempts by companies to "police" online use of IP (often referred to as "cyberbullying") have clashed with the free speech culture of the Internet. Dilution of a trademark occurs when "the capacity of a famous mark to identify and distinguish goods or services (Lanham Trademark Act, 1946, § 1127)" is lessened, for example, when an identifiable mark is used without permission on a commercial Web site. (Noncommercial use of a mark, comparative commercial advertising, and news commentary are exceptions to the usual dilution standards (§ 1125).) Current trademark law requires companies to "police" some forms of unauthorized use of trademarks in order to protect the fame of their mark and show that they have not abandoned it (§ 1115; § 1127). If they fail to control how others use their marks, they run the risk of the marks being used generically, as "common use" words, such as "jello" (rather than Jell-O brand gelatin dessert), "kleenex" (rather than "Kleenex tissue"), and "band-aid" (rather than "Band-Aid brand adhesive bandage"). Even when use of a trademark name does not rise to the level of common use, the mark may still lose its power to associate the trademark holder's goods with the trademark holder, and the company may lose trademark protection for that mark altogether (§ 1115; § 1125).

The Culture of the Internet and the Application of IP Law

A recent article entitled "Culture Wars on the Net" (Coombe and Herman, 2001) discussed corporate practices of policing trademarks on the Internet and cited efforts by Coca-Cola to suppress the online use of their trademarks as a form of online censorship. Coca-Cola had taken action against a Web site that was donated to senior citizens who collected and traded vintage Coca-Cola bottles and cans. The site, called Vintagecoca-cola.com, was used to display the seniors' collections. In January 2000, the site's administrator received a cease-and-desist letter from Coca-Cola with instructions to "discontinue use of all Coca-Cola trademarks and to assign the domain name to the company or abandon it (p. 925)." Despite the fact that the site contained appropriate disclaimers (and the seniors never sold the products that they displayed), the group relinquished the site. Company actions to stop *modifications* of product images have also been challenged by the Internet community as attempts to control, or censor, Internet expression. In 1997, for example, Mattel took action against the creator of a Web site who had posted "texts and visuals, including alterations to the [image of a Barbie] doll's face, to explore the role of the doll as an icon of American life (p. 932)." The Internet community criticized Mattel's actions as "incredible blatant censorship (p. 933)," and reacted by posting numerous Barbie sites with a variety of themes and images.

Presenting a social perspective of this issue, Naomi Klein argued in her 1999 book, *No Logo*, that "such examples [of cyberbullying] give a picture of corporate space as a fascist state where we all salute the logo and have little opportunity for criticism because our newspapers, television stations, Internet servers, streets and retail spaces are all controlled by multinational corporate interests (p. 187)." On the other hand, it is evident from studies in product marketing that the value of many products, as perceived by consumers, increasingly has been derived from "the brand experience as a lifestyle (p. 27)," resulting in increased corporate expenditures on the development and marketing of product *concepts* and increased corporate efforts to protect product *concepts* (along with decreased expenditures in the production of the physical product). This evidence leads to a question about the true beneficiary of strong IPR protections: Are strong IPR protections a product of corporate interests (leveraged by substantial political influence) or national interests (representing the population-at-large)?

Internet-related copyright violations of IP such as music, movies, and software have also received a great deal of public attention in recent years. Although these violations allegedly impact industry revenues directly, there is no clear consensus that the long-term economic effects of such violations undermine innovation and economic development. In fact, precisely the opposite has been argued: that in the absence of monopolistic control, innovation is stimulated, rates of production increase, marginal production costs decrease, and revenue increases (assuming that demand increases disproportionately to price decreases, as should be the case with elastic goods such as music, movies, and software) (Boldrin and Levine, 2003). One of the most convincing illustrations of this theory is the open source software "movement," which began in its present form in 1998. The premise of this movement is that free distribution of software and its source codes stimulates the creation of new knowledge through the open sharing of ideas and their associated products. Among the most widely recognized products produced through the open source concept—which is responsible for in excess of 50,000 projects—is the GNU/Linux operating system and Apache server software (Von Hippel and Von Krogh, 2003).

In the music industry, however, the Recording Industry Association of America (RIAA) has articulated a strong position against IPR violations and began an "education and enforcement campaign" in 2003 that resulted in "more than 1,500 subpoenas and nearly 350 lawsuits" against individual computer users found "sharing" music in peer-to-peer (P2P) networks (Lyman, 2003). Although representatives of the RIAA have called this campaign successful, critics have argued that "suing your customers is not a winning strategy (Shell, 2003)." G. Richard Shell (2003), a Wharton legal studies professor, identified the problem as one of public legitimacy and described a significant distinction between an attack on a distributor such as Napster and an attack on "otherwise law-abiding consumers who download music." The danger of ignoring this distinction, he wrote, was illustrated 100 years ago, "when leading automobile manufacturers in 1903 tried to put down the threat of cheap, mass-produced cars by suing consumers who bought Henry Ford's automobiles." The battle in the automobile industry culminated with a shift in public sympathy and a barrage of editorials that deemed the industry's lawsuits against consumers heavy-handed. To some extent, the RIAA's actions have been met with similar responses. The infamous lawsuit against a twelve-year-old girl in New York for downloading songs is one example.

In an effort to accommodate potential benefits of freely distributed IP over the Internet, Canada has implemented a private copying exemption that permits individuals to copy musical works for private use and uses taxes levied against blank recording products to compensate artists for potential losses from this practice (Canadian Intellectual Property Office, 1998). In 1992, the U.S. adopted a "prohibition on certain infringement actions (Audio Home Recording Act, §1008)" that bears some similarity to the Canadian law; however, the U.S. law applies only to devises whose *primary* purpose is "making a digital audio copied recording for private use (§1001)," that is, it does not apply to audio recordings downloaded to a computer. In Canada, downloading music from peer-to-peer networks is permitted (Borland, 2003). One argument that supports the Canadian strategy is that a private copying exemption allows law enforcement to allocate more resources to IPR violations that represent a greater threat to IP development. Studies of alternative IP laws in Canada and other countries may help to identify consequences—whether intended or unintended—of IP laws and enforcement practices and increase our understanding of successful means of stimulating IP innovation and economic growth.

IPR Violations from an International Perspective

Since U.S.-based IP constitutes a major portion of IP available worldwide, application of U.S. IP law outside of the U.S. has become a subject of serious debate. There is, for example, a strong sentiment in U.S. law that "legislation ... is meant to apply only within the territorial jurisdiction of the United States (*Foley Bros. v. Filardo*, 1949)." To the extent that U.S. law is applicable abroad, the doctrine ("Restatement of the Law," 1987) of "substantial effect" is often used. This doctrine establishes that "a state has jurisdiction to prescribe law with respect to ... conduct outside its territory that has or is intended to have substantial effect within its territory." Specifically, the U.S. Supreme Court has held that U.S. law "applies to foreign conduct that was meant to produce and did in fact produce some substantial effect in the United States (*Hartford Fire Ins. Co. v. California*, 1993)." Taken broadly, this doctrine (of substantial effect) gives the U.S. justification for applying its laws to acts that occur wholly between foreign nationals in a foreign country in accordance to that country's laws, so long as the acts affect the United States. Needless to say, U.S. attempts to apply this doctrine have been challenged.

Given the debate over this matter, application of IP law to activities outside of the U.S. are decided on a case-by case basis by judges whose socio-political perspectives may vary widely and who may assign different values to competing interests. To help minimize this variability, a number of U.S. agencies have recently established significant relationships with foreign and international organizations. Since 2002, the National Intellectual Property Rights Coordination Center (IPR Center), formed by the Federal Bureau of Investigation (FBI) and the Immigration and Customs Enforcement (ICE), has had substantial success coordinating IP efforts in the U.S. with those in other countries, as well as coordinating law enforcement efforts with those of IP-based industries. International agencies engaged in activities with the IPR Center include the International Criminal Police Organization (Interpol), the World Intellectual Property Organization (WIPO), and the World Trade Organization (WTO). Other U.S. agencies that are actively involved in IP information exchange and enforcement efforts include the U.S. Department of State, Bureau of Economic and Business Affairs, and the U.S. Commerce Department. Non-governmental organizations that advance enforcement of IPR violations include the International Intellectual Property Alliance (IIPA), International AntiCounterfeiting Coalition (IACC), Recording Industry Association of America (RIIA), Business Software Alliance (BSA), Motion Picture Association of America (MPAA), and Pharmaceutical Security Institute Inc. (PSI).

Despite these efforts, the effectiveness and likelihood of bilateral or multilateral cooperative agreements tend to vary widely from country to country. In addition, violators of IPR have shown a willingness to relocate their activities to countries without a good working relationship with U.S. law enforcement or the ability to effectively enforce IP laws.

Research on IPR Violations

Currently, the cumulative information on IPR violations consists primarily of estimates of economic losses to specific industries or legal action by specific groups. For example, the Business Software Alliance (BSA) has published studies on software piracy that estimates the amount of business application software installed without a license throughout the world. Worldwide, BSA has estimated that the highest software piracy rates existed in Vietnam (95 percent) and China (92 percent) in 2002, and the lowest rates were found in the U.S. (23 percent) and New Zealand (24 percent). The greatest dollar losses for 2002 were shown in China ($2.4 billion) and the U.S. (almost $2 billion). Overall, the worldwide software piracy rate has declined somewhat since 1994 (from 49 percent to 39 percent), while the worldwide economic loss (in U.S. dollars) has increased slightly (from $12.3 billion to $13 billion) (Business Software Alliance, 2003a). Within the U.S., the highest software piracy rates were found in Mississippi (41.7 percent) and Wyoming (40.3 percent), and the lowest rates were found in Illinois (13.5 percent) and Michigan (13.9 percent). The greatest dollar losses were in California ($241 million) and Florida ($122 million) (Business Software Alliance,

2003b). The nation-wide piracy rate in 2002 was eight percent lower than the rate in 1994, a drop from 31 to 23 percent (Business Software Alliance, 2003a). An interesting complement to these data is WIPO's (2002) estimates of Internet penetration. In 2002, the areas with a high percent of Internet use were in Sweden (64.6 percent), Denmark (60.3 percent), Hong Kong, China (59.6 percent), and the U.S. (59.2 percent).

A survey by the International Intellectual Property Alliance (IIPA) (2003), a coalition that represents U.S. copyright-based industries, found piracy rates that were consistent with BSA's findings, though the dollar losses associated with these rates differed somewhat. The IIPA survey also provided statistics on losses in the motion picture, recording, and entertainment software industries. For example, China's piracy rates for each of these industries were reported as 91, 90, and 96 percent respectively.

By most accounts, the rate of IPR violations has not significantly changed worldwide in the past five years; however, the estimated dollar losses continue to increase, as does the quality of counterfeited goods being distributed. Countries identified as those with the largest volume of illegal IP activity include China, Russia, Ukraine, Vietnam, Taiwan, Pakistan, and Indonesia.

U.S. data on law enforcement efforts to reduce IP crime, reported by U.S. Customs and Border Protection (Customs), show that the number of IP seizures worldwide in 2003 exceeded the levels of the previous five years (n.d. a; n.d. b). The value of Customs' 2003 IP seizures was estimated at $94 million, a slight decrease from the $99 million seized in 2002 (United States Customs and Border Protection, 2004). The FBI's IP crime deterrence efforts have produced 92 indictments and 95 convictions for 2003, following 121 indictments and seventy-six convictions in 2002. Neither of the two most recent years, however, reaches the collective 2001 levels, which included 114 indictments and 177 convictions (United States Department of Justice, 2004). The FBI (2002) has estimated overall losses to U.S. businesses from IP crime at $200 to $250 billion per year. Estimates of losses worldwide are about twice this figure (Organization for Economic Co-operation and Development, 1998). These overall figures represent not only estimates for goods such as software, music, and movies; they also represent counterfeit goods such as cigarettes, apparel, perfumes, electronics, and pharmaceuticals.

The NW3C IPR Study

The issues and concerns that have been discussed in this report thus far represent not only subjects of debate in academic and legal environments but also matters of practical significance for law enforcement, prosecutors, policy makers, and IP-based industries, as well as the general public, whose daily lives are affected by IP in a variety of ways. To gain some insight into the application of IP laws, NW3C conducted interviews with law enforcement and IP-based industry representatives and administered surveys to law enforcement, prosecutors, trade association investigators and attorneys, IP-based business representatives, and private attorneys. This study not only elicited responses to pointed questions about the nature and consequences of IPR violations but also invited open discussion and explanation of obstacles, needs, and concerns.

The most prominent theme of discussion in the NW3C study was inadequate support, coordination, and education in the area of IPR and enforcement efforts. All of those interviewed indicated that training of investigators, prosecutors, judges, and the general public was a pressing need, as well as developing methods for building on-going cooperative efforts between law enforcement and businesses for the exchange of information. Although law enforcement reported that industry was much better educated than in previous years, and industry reported that investigators were taking IPR violations more seriously than several years ago, education at the state- and local-levels for law enforcement, prosecutors, and the public was reported as inadequate. Even with most IPR enforcement occurring at the federal level, this education was identified as crucial to enable state and local law enforcement to know what to look for and how to handle IPR violations. Specifically, 84 percent of respondents stated that investigators lack adequate training in IP issues, and 53 percent indicated that prosecutors typically fail to take IPR violations seriously. In response to this problem, both federal agencies and IP-based industries have extended training opportunities to state and local law enforcement (Organization for Economic Co-operation and Development, 1998). Not surprisingly, inadequate resources for IP cases were identified by 74 percent of respondents as an obstacle.

Communication, Coordination and Cooperative Efforts

The interviews and other queries of NW3C indicated that substantial progress has been made in recent years with respect to adjusting policies to accommodate changes in technology, providing education in IP issues, and coordinating efforts in IPR enforcement. As with many areas of law enforcement and regulation, some of the most challenging obstacles to success involve jurisdictional constraints, information restrictions, and interests of autonomy. On both the national (U.S.) and international levels, these three obstacles are inevitably related. For instance, in the U.S., agencies at local, state, and federal levels tend to protect rather than share information concerning their activities, which tends to intensify jurisdictional limitations and impede resolution of IP problems. The same occurs among agencies in different countries, with the added complication, in many cases, of substantial differences in law, culture, and economic interests. Finally, communication with those who represent IP consumers, including consumers of illegally created IP, has been limited. One example of such an effort that was deemed successful was described in a NW3C interview. Federal law enforcement provided an online forum for discussion and debate on the subject of IP and online IP violations. This communication not only afforded online consumers an opportunity to ask questions, express objections, and gain knowledge about IP issues, it also provided law enforcement with a better understanding of consumer IP concerns and Internet culture.

A substantial concern of many respondents was the absence of IP laws in many countries and the failure of countries with existing IP laws to enforce those laws. In addition, most respondents (74 percent) indicated that better information about foreign laws would be a valuable tool, along with contact information for foreign law enforcement. To some extent, it was reported that these problems are in the early stages of resolution. The FBI, for example, described significant and on-going cooperative efforts with Interpol, WIPO, WPO, and industry representatives. Currently, the IP Crime Action Group, coordinated by Interpol, is working to develop a model for adoption by all countries. In addition, a steering committee, with members representing all regions of the world, is working to establish training initiatives. Another effort designed to provide training and assistance in IP crime is the IPR Training Coordination Group, sponsored by the Bureau of Economic and Business Affairs of the U.S. Department of State. Comprised of U.S. government agencies and IP-based industry associations, this group extends training and assistance to foreign officials and policy makers around the world

(United States Department of State, n.d.). Clearly coordination on such a large scale requires willingness and ability to manage significant differences in cultures, norms, and traditions. Continued participation in these efforts by U.S. representatives, including law enforcement and industry, was reported as important for addressing both U.S. and global IP concerns.

Another concern, which is related to inconsistencies in IP laws and enforcement around the world, is the prevalence of non-traditional, transnational organized crime groups associated with IP crime. Several respondents noted that an increasing number of pirating groups are basing their operations abroad. Because of the difficulties inherent in coordinating law enforcement efforts in multiple countries and the lack of IP laws and enforcement in some countries, this trend is likely to continue. Although a great deal of study has been devoted to activities of traditional organized crime groups in the past, limited information is available about groups that are organized in a nontraditional way or engage in activities that are not historically typical of organized crime groups. In addition, new and creative techniques for counterfeiting or pirating goods, which are often the product of organized criminal efforts, are reported as difficult to stay abreast of. Although 95 percent of respondents indicated that information about new techniques was valuable, 84 percent indicated that the information was either unavailable or inadequate.

With respect to IP enforcement within the U.S., varying opinions were expressed in the NW3C study about federal- and state-level IP coordination specific to jurisdiction and authority. Federal law enforcement and IP-based industry representatives suggested that a system should be established to facilitate uniformity of laws among states and to encourage more states to develop IP laws. Clarifying the jurisdictional authority of state and federal agencies and courts would also be required in this situation. (Currently, federal patent, copyright, and trademark law preempts state law, in most instances, even when a state has laws to specifically address IP.) One argument for this recommendation (articulated by respondents) was that state and local law enforcement tend to have a better understanding of and access to local problems and needs. Other respondents expressed concern that some IP cases fail to meet dollar thresholds (of losses) set for acceptance as federal cases and therefore are never addressed. Given adequate funding and education for state and local law enforcement, this recommendation could also serve to relieve federal law enforcement of responsibility for smaller cases and allow states to address cases that cannot be handled at the federal level. A state regulator and private attorney interviewed by NW3C, on the other hand, felt that all IP issues should be addressed at the federal level. The primary argument for this suggestion was that there are too many exceptions to the law, too many inconsistencies in court rulings, and a general lack of understanding of IP law.

A few respondents, from the software industry and state law enforcement, expressed a desire for new laws that could directly address specific concerns. Potential laws that were mentioned included Internet laws, peer-to-peer piracy laws, laws requiring Internet Service Providers (ISPs) to provide information about suspected IPR violators, and protection for whistle-blowers. However, federal law enforcement respondents indicated that it might not be useful to create new laws to address IP. It might be more useful to modify existing laws—on a regular basis. In addition, federal law enforcement respondents indicated that industry should bear the primary responsibility for addressing their specific IPR problems, using law enforcement only as a last resort.

Conclusion

Despite the numerous and disparate views on the extent to which producers of IP should be economically protected and the public should have access to IP, there is little argument that some forms of IP misappropriation results in harm to the public. In addition to physical harm from counterfeited products such as medical supplies, vehicle parts, and tools, IP violations can contribute to substantial economic harm to consumers—through fraudulent representations of company affiliation or product value (e.g., investment fraud), or unauthorized use of personal information (e.g., identity theft)—and to businesses. IP violations have also been found to be funding sources for violent harm, such as terrorist activities.

Major challenges that obstruct efforts to reduce this harm, include increasingly sophisticated technology for reproduction (including the Internet), increasing activities in global commerce and communication, and significant differences in social and legal norms throughout the world. To address these challenges, it seems necessary to develop some understanding, if not agreement, about how IP should be used (i.e., protected, distributed, and shared) that is applicable in a multi-national context and attentive not only to the interests of IP holders but also to the interests of potential IP users. It also seems prudent to recognize that as technologies become increasingly sophisticated and social responsibility increasingly becomes a global matter, it may be necessary to reevaluate some uses of IP that have been denied or restricted in the past. Evaluation of policy and development of some foundational understanding is likely to require extensive and on-going dialogue among a variety of communities. Without this kind of systemic dialogue, conflicting views and behaviors will likely continue to undermine at least some of the goals of every group with an interest in IP.

Notes

1. The Universal Declaration of Human Rights, adopted by the General Assembly of the United Nations, has recognized protections of intellectual property as a universal human right. However, definitions and applications related to IP continue to be a matter of controversy, as does the very basis for the UN declaration.
2. These data, for all years reported, include both indictments and information.
3. These data, for all years reported, include convictions and pre-trial diversions.
4. Additional information available at http://www.interpol.int/Public/FinancialCrime/ IntellectualProperty/ Default.asp.

References

Arrow, K.J. (1962). Economic welfare and the allocation of resources for invention. In Nelson, R. (Ed.), *The rate and direction of inventive activity* (pp. 609-625). Princeton, NJ: Princeton University Press.

Audio Home Recording Act, 17 U.S.C. § 1001 et seq. (1992).

Bessen, J. and Maskin, E. (2000, January). *Sequential innovation, patents, and imitation.* [Working Paper], Massachusetts Institute of Technology, Department of Economics. Retrieved October 10, 2003, from http://www.researchoninnovation.org/patent.pdf.

Boldrin, M. and Levine, D.K. (2003, January). *Perfectly competitive innovation.* [Working Paper], University of Minnesota and University of California, Los Angeles. Retrieved April 29, 2005, from http://www.dklevine.com/papers/pci23.pdf.

Borland, J. (2003, December 15). Canada: Downloading music is legal. *CNET News.com.* Retrieved March 19, 2004, from http://news.zdnet.co.uk/business/legal/0,39020651,39118537,00.htm.

Business Software Alliance (BSA). (2003a, June). *Eighth annual BSA global software piracy study: trends in software piracy 1994-2002.* International Planning and Research Corporation.

Business Software Alliance (BSA). (2003b, August). *2002 U.S. software: State piracy study.* International Planning and Research Corporation.

Canadian Intellectual Property Office (CIPO). (1998, March 19). *Circular no. 15: Private copying, strategis.gc.ca.* Retrieved January 12, 2004, from http://strategis. gc.ca/sc_mrksv/cipo/cp/cp_circ_15-e.html.

Coombe, R.J. and Herman, A. (2001). Culture wars on the net: Intellectual property and corporate propriety in digital environments. *The South Atlantic Quarterly, 100(4),* 919-947.

ETHICON, Inc. (2003, October 28). Counterfeit phone alert. Retrieved February 25, 2004, from http://www.ethicon.com/notice.html.

The criminalization of copyright infringement in the digital era. (1999). *Harvard Law Review, 112(7),* 1705-1722.

Feist Publications v. Rural Tel. Serv. Co., 499 U.S. 340,349 (1991).

Foley Bros., Inc. v. Filardo, 336 U.S. 281, 285, 93 L. Ed. 680, 69 S. Ct. 575 (1949).

Hartford Fire Ins. Co. v. California, 509 U.S. 764 (1993).

International Intellectual Property Alliance (IIPA). (2003, November). USTR 2003 'special 301' decisions on intellectual property. Retrieved February 12, 2004, from http://www.iipa.com/pdf/2003_Nov_USTR_LossUpd.pdf.

Kamal, M. and Bailey, M. (2003, July 26). TRIPS: Whose interests are being served? *The Lancet, 362,* 260.

Kanwar, S. and Evenson, R.E. (2001, June). *Does intellectual property protection spur technological change?(Yale University).* New Haven, CT: Economic Growth Center.

Klein, N. (1999). *No logo: Taking aim at the brand bullies.* New York: Picador.

Lanham Trademark Act, 15 U.S.C.§ 1115 et seq. (1946).

Lee, H.K. (2001, February 28). Salesman caught in trade show sting: Vendor accused of hiding profits. *San Francisco Chronicle.* Retrieved February 24, 2003, from http://www.sfgate.com/cgi-bin/article.cgi?file=/chronicle/archive/2001/02/28/MNW87715.DTL.

Los Angeles Police Department. (2003, September 12). Major brand counterfeiting ring broken. Retrieved February 24, 2004, from http://www.lapdonline.org/press_releases/2003/09/pr03667.htm.

Lyman, J. (2003, November 3). RIAA second wave of suits hits file traders, more to come. *TechNewsWorld.com.* Retrieved January 23, 2004, from http://www.ecommercetimes.com/perl/story/32021.html.

Mazer v. Stein, 347 U.S. 201, 209 (1954).

Money Laundering Control Act, 18 U.S.C. § 1956 (1988).

Nigeria reaffirms efforts to eliminate fake drugs. (2003, February 13). *Xinhua General News* Service.

Organization for Economic Co-operation and Development. (1998). The economic impact of counterfeiting. Retrieved February 22, 2004, from http://www.oecd.org/dataoecd/11/11/2090589.pdf.

Ostergard, R.L. (1999). Intellectual property: A universal human right? *Human Rights Quarterly, 21(1),* 156-178.

Restatement of the law, third, foreign relations law of the United States. (1987). *The American Law Institute, Sec. 403,* Reporters Note 1.

Romer, P. (1990). Are nonconvexities important for understanding growth? *The American Economic Review(Papers and Proceedings), 80,* 97-103.

Sen, A. (1996). Goods and people. In W. Aiken and H. LaFollette (Eds.), *World hunger and morality.* Upper Saddle River, NJ: Prentice Hall.

Shell, R.G. (2003, October 22). Suing your customers: A winning business strategy? *Strategic Management.* Retrieved January 23, 2004, from http://knowledge.wharton.upenn.edu/index.cfm?fa=printArticleandID=863.

Stern, B. (1996, June 10). Warning! Bogus parts have turned up in commercial jets. Where is the FAA? *Business Week,* 90.

Sutherland, E.H. (1983). *White collar crime: The uncut version.* New Haven, CT: Yale University Press. (Originally published 1949).

U.S. Bank hit by international hackers: Counterfeit ring hacks Nebraska bank's computer. (2003, July 24). *Online Security.* Retrieved February 25, 2004, from http://www.onlinesecurity.com/links456.php.

United States Customs and Border Protection (CBP). (n.d. a). Seizure data. Retrieved February 11, 2004, from http://www.cbp.gov/xp/cgov/import/commercial_enforcement/ipr/seizure/seizure_stats.xml.

United States Customs and Border Protection (CBP). (n.d. b). Yearly comparisons: Seizure statistics for intellectual property rights (mid-year FY 2003). Retrieved February 11, 2004, from http://www.cbp.gov/xp/cgov/import/commercial_enforcement/ipr/seizure/seizure_stats.xml.

United States Customs and Border Protection (CBP). (2004, January 14). U.S. Customs and Border Protection announces intellectual property rights seizure data [Press Release]. Retrieved February 11, 2004, from http://www.cbp.gov/xp/cgov/newsroom/press_releases/01142004_5.xml.

United States Department of Justice. (2004, January 28). Data presented at a meeting, Washington DC.

United States Department of Justice, Federal Bureau of Investigation (FBI). (2002, July 17). The Federal Bureau of Investigation and the U.S. Customs Service today announced the National Intellectual Property Rights Coordination Center's first conference for members of Congress and Industry in Washington DC [Press Release]. Retrieved February 11, 2004, from http://www.fbi.gov/pressrel/pressrel02/outreach071702.htm.

United States Department of Justice, United States Attorney. (2001, March 6). Silicon valley businessman pleads guilty to hiding proceeds of sales of counterfeit computer software [Press Release]. Retrieved February 24, 2004 from http://www.cybercrime.gov/dingPlea.htm.

United States Department of State, Bureau of Economic and Business Affairs. (n.d.) Intellectual property rights training program database. Available at http://www.training.ipr.gov.

United States Security and Exchange Commission. (1999, August 30). Litigation release no. 16266. Retrieved February 20, 2004, from http://www.sec.gov/litigation/litreleases/lr16266.htm.

Von Hippel, E. and Von Krogh, G. (2003). Open source software and the 'private-collective' innovation model: Issues for organization science. *Organization Science, 14(2),* 209-223. Retrieved September 12, 2004, from http://web.mit.edu/evhippel/wwwPrivateCollectiveWP.pdf.

World Intellectual Property Organization (WIPO). (2002, December). Intellectual property on the internet: A survey of issues. Retrieved September 16, 2003, from http://www.ecomerce.wipo.int/survey.

5

Addressing the Global Scope of Intellectual Property Crimes and Policy Initiatives

Hedieh Nasheri
Kent State University

Introduction

Intellectual property (IP) is a growing concern in both the criminal and civil justice systems due to the growing number of products that can be reproduced quickly and inexpensively with little chance of detection. The economic impact of the misuse and theft of intellectual property is far-reaching.[1] The copying of software, movies, video games, and music in ways that deny publishers and authors their legal rights have drawn the most attention, but trademark and patent infringement, corporate espionage, computer intrusions, theft and sale of trade secrets, and international smuggling and transmission of copyrighted materials also have been identified as problems.

The National Institute of Justice sponsored several studies to examine the nature of this problem, to discover what is known about its extent and the major justice-related issues it creates, and to develop recommendations for future research in this area. As part of its International Center's research agenda to enhance understanding of intellectual property crimes (IPC) and its implications for practice, funding was provided to analyze the current state of law and enforcement efforts for protection of intellectual property rights (IPRs), and its actual and potential uses.[2]

This article represents an assessment of the "state of the art," as well as concrete evidence of weaknesses in current law, in its enforcement domestically and internationally, in problems of application and training, and in other matters that can be used to assist researchers in this untapped area. While the broader interest of the NIJ project was to examine the policy issues associated with protection and enforcement of IPRs, the results provide a starting point for a critical analysis of the current state of laws, law enforcement, and potential threats of IPC in a global context. This study is not intended to provide solutions to all the problems that it identifies but, rather, raises policy considerations for further research and legislative initiatives.

Research Methodology

Two research methods were used for this study:

A.   Archival Review – An extensive review was conducted of federal regulations, case reports, journal articles, speeches, testimony, arrest records, indictments, court records, GAO reports, Congressional hearings reports, agency reports, seminar reports and newspaper articles.

B.   Primary Source Interviews – Interviews were conducted with selected interest groups, including corporate security professionals, security consultants and federal prosecutors, other government officials in the Department of Justice, and the FBI who play key roles in prosecution and investigation of criminal activities in this area.

What is Intellectual Property?

IP is the term that describes the ideas, inventions, technologies, artworks, music and literature, that are intangible, but typically are rendered into valuable and tangible products. The word "property" is used to describe this value, because the term applies to inventions, works and names for which a person or group of persons claims ownership. Ownership in this context is important because the prospect of potential economic gain provides a powerful incentive to innovate. IP, very broadly, involves the legal rights that result from intellectual activity in the industrial, scientific, literary and artistic fields.

According to the World Intellectual Property Organization (WIPO), IP shall include rights relating to the following:

- literary, artistic and scientific works,
- performances of performing artists, phonograms, and broadcasts,
- inventions in all fields of human endeavor,
- scientific discoveries,

- industrial designs,
- trademarks, service marks, and commercial names and designations,
- protection against unfair competition,
- and all other rights resulting from intellectual activity in the industrial, scientific, literary or artistic fields."[3]

Protectable property interests are present in both real property and IP. Real property is a commonly understood concept; it is any physical or tangible property, such as a house, a watch, or a piece of land.[4] IP, on the other hand, is not usually something you can touch, but it exists and has the same value. Copyrights, patents, trademarks and trade secrets are all forms of IP.[5] IPRs refers to the legal rights that correspond to intellectual activity in the industrial, scientific, and artistic fields. These legal rights, most commonly in the form of patents, trademarks, and copyright, protect the moral and economic rights of the creators, in addition to the creativity and dissemination of their work.

Different Categories of Intellectual Property

IP is divided into two categories: industrial property and copyright.[6] Industrial property extends protection to inventions and industrial designs. Industrial property includes patents, trademarks, industrial design, and geographic indications of source.[7] Whereas copyright protects literary and artistic works such as novels, poems, plays, films, musical works, drawings, paintings, photographs, sculptures, software, and architectural designs.[8]

Industrial Property

Industrial property rights make it possible for the creators of innovations (goods, processes, apparatus, etc.) to establish themselves more readily, to penetrate new markets with a minimum of risk, and to amortize the investments made in the research that led to the innovations in the first place. In a practical sense, these innovations become the spearhead of some of the most advanced technology.

Patent (Invention). A patent is an exclusive right granted for an invention (a product or a process that provides a new way of doing something, or offers a new technical solution to a problem). It provides protection for the invention for a limited period, generally twenty years from the filing date, in the country or countries in which it is patented, in exchange for the inventor's public disclosure of the invention.

Trademark. A trademark or "mark" is a distinctive name, logo or sign[9] identifying the source of goods or services. Trademarks help consumers distinguish a product or service from one source from those produced by another source. A mark provides protection to its owner by preventing confusion as to source in connection with the distribution of goods or services or licensing others to use them. The period of protection varies, but a mark can remain valid indefinitely through continued commercial use or a registration and renewal process.

Copyright and Related Rights

Copyright consists of a bundle of rights given to creators in their literary and artistic works. These creators, and their heirs, hold the exclusive rights to use or license others to use the work on agreed terms. The creator of a work can prohibit or authorize,[10] for example:

- its reproduction in various forms, such as a printed publication or a phonograph record;
- its public performance, as in a play or musical work;
- its broadcasting, including by radio, television, or satellite;
- its translation into other languages, or its adaptation, such as the adaptation of a novel into a screenplay.

Copyright applies to many different types of artistic works, including paintings, music, poems, plays, books, architecture and choreography, as well as to works that are generally not considered artistic such as computer software, maps and technical drawings. Related rights are rights that have evolved in the last fifty years or so around copyright, and include the right of a performer in his/her performance, the right of a producer of a sound recording in the recording, and the right of a broadcaster in a broadcast.

Many creative works protected by copyright generally require mass distribution, communication, and financial investment for their dissemination (for example, publications, sound recordings, and films). Hence, creators often sell the rights to their works to individuals or companies that can package, market, and distribute the works in return for payment (lump sum or royalties). These economic rights have a time limit according to the relevant WIPO treaty of the life of the author plus fifty years after the author's death. In some countries that term has been extended to seventy years. Copyright may also include moral rights which involve the right to claim authorship of a work and the right to oppose changes to it that could harm the creator's reputation.

IPRs have come to occupy an increasingly important position in international trade and development. The importance of IPRs has led to the inclusion of IP provisions in international agreements and treaties. IP in itself has always been an integral part of general economic, social and cultural development worldwide, but new challenges emphasize all the more how globally interlinked national and regional IP systems have become.

IP theft is now one of the foremost international concerns that affect global economies and governments. Although not as high-profile as terrorism, smuggling, human and drug trafficking, infringement and counterfeiting have been feared to weaken legitimate business systems that would result in international economic disasters.[11]

Intellectual Property Crimes and Organized Crime

IPC are serious crimes in their own right, not typically because they inflict physical injury or death upon a person, but rather because they steal a creative work from its owner.[12] IPC refers to counterfeited and pirated goods, manufactured and sold for profit without the consent of the patent or trademark holder.[13] The terms "piracy" and "counterfeiting" are often used interchangeably. However, piracy is generally related to the theft of IPRs by some form of copying the original.[14] Whereas, counterfeiting is the copying of a product's trademark or the distinctive way the package looks.[15] IPC involve a wide range of criminal actors ranging from individuals to organized criminal groups and terrorist organizations.

There is now a strong belief that there is an even greater threat posed by the organizations involved in counterfeiting and piracy. IPC includes the manufacturing, transporting, storing, and sale of counterfeit or pirated goods. Organized crime involvement in the manufacture, distribution, and sale of counterfeit and pirated merchandise is no longer denied. The increasing involvement of organized crime in the production and distribution of pirated products further complicates enforcement efforts. Federal and foreign law enforcement officials have linked intellectual property crime to national and transnational organized criminal operations. According to the Secretary General of Interpol, intellectual property crime is now dominated by criminal organizations, and law enforcement authorities have identified some direct and some alleged links between intellectual property crime and paramilitary and terrorist groups.[16] Justice Department officials noted that they are aware of the allegations linking intellectual property crime and terrorist funding and that they are actively exploring all potential avenues of terrorist financing, including through intellectual property crime. However, to date, U.S. law enforcement has not found solid evidence that intellectual property has been or is being pirated in the United States by or for the benefit of terrorists. The involvement of organized crime increases the sophistication of counterfeiting operations, as well as the challenges and threats to law enforcement officials confronting the violations. Moreover, according to officials in Brazil, organized criminal activity surrounding intellectual property crime is linked with official corruption, which can pose an additional obstacle to U.S. and foreign efforts to promote enhanced enforcement.

Future Economic Crime Risks

Few sources exist that report comprehensive and seemingly reliable data on the extent of the problem. The two principle studies chosen for use in this report are studies by PricewaterhouseCoopers and the Brookings Institute due to their quality reputations and the apparent thoroughness of the reports. An independent audit and scrutiny of the data they report is, of course, beyond the scope of this study.

According to the PricewaterhouseCoopers' 2003 *Economic Crime Survey,* economic crime is, and will remain, a costly issue. It is, however, an issue that can be countered by effective controls, a strong culture of prevention and deterrence and assertive action when cases arise.

Over the course of the past two decades, IP owners have witnessed an explosion in the levels of counterfeiting and piracy, in both the domestic and international arenas. IP theft is rampant but largely silent so corporations and law enforcement alike have trouble grasping its enormous impact on profitability—not to mention on national economies.[17,18] Because counterfeiting and piracy are illegal, many of the normal elements associated with legitimate business are removed, and as a result, benefits are denied society at different levels. Initially, loss of direct sales revenues is experienced by legitimate manufacturers. The size of such loss is monumental, often beyond our comprehension.

It is difficult to get an accurate overview of the worldwide magnitude of the IP theft problem. Those who commit acts of counterfeiting and piracy generally do not file official reports on their sales. Seizures affect only a percentage of the overall market, and the extent of counterfeiting and piracy, including that which occurs in businesses, homes, and in private situations, may never be known with certainty.

Counterfeiting and piracy likewise have damaging consequences for consumers. They generally involve deliberately deceiving the consumer about the quality he is entitled to expect from a product bearing, for example, a well-known trademark. When he buys counterfeit or pirated goods outside the legitimate trade, the consumer does not ordinarily receive any after-sales service or enjoy any effective recourse in the event of damage or injury.

Counterfeiting and piracy also has an adverse effect upon public security, where profits from this trade are appropriated by organized crime, which uses them as a means of recycling and laundering the proceeds of other unlawful activities (e.g. arms, drugs, etc.).

Magnitude of the Problem

Counterfeiting and digital piracy have increased dramatically in recent years and are areas of particular concern.[19] Unfortunately, in the area of counterfeiting what was once a localized industry concentrated on the copying of high-end designer goods has now become a massive, sophisticated global business involving the manufacturing and sale of counterfeit versions of everything from soaps, shampoos, razors and batteries to cigarettes, alcoholic beverages and automobile parts, as well as medicines and health care products.

Counterfeiting of such a broad range of products on a global scale affects more than just the companies that produce legitimate products. While it has a direct impact on the sales and profits of those companies, counterfeits also hurt the consumers who waste their money and sometimes put themselves at risk by purchasing fake goods. It also hurts the countries concerned by decreasing tax revenues and deterring investments. In addition, counterfeiters pay no taxes or duties and do not comply with basic manufacturing standards for the health and safety of workers or product quality and performance.

Piracy and counterfeiting of copyrighted products in digital, print (e.g., books, journals, and other printed materials) and other analogue formats, as well as counterfeiting of all types of trademarked products, have grown to such a scale because these illegal activities offer enormous profits and little risk for the criminal element of society. Criminals can get into the counterfeiting business with little capital investment and, even if caught and charged with a crime, the penalties imposed in many countries are so low that they offer no deterrent.[20]

Most people when confronted with the problem of counterfeit and pirated products generally conjure up images of products typically peddled by sidewalk vendors—music CDs, sunglasses, t-shirts, hats, cosmetics, cell phone covers, handbags, and watches—bearing easily recognizable and well known names, marks, and logos. Modern day counterfeiting operations, however, are no longer limited to luxury goods and apparel-related products. On a more sophisticated and organized level, counterfeiters and pirates are also trading on names and logos often associated with products like razor blades, shampoos, pharmaceuticals, foods, hand tools, auto parts, airline parts, light bulbs, film, skin lotions, laundry detergent, insecticides, batteries, cigarettes, and practically anything else that bears a name that consumers recognize. As infringers become more brazen and as technology provides them with the ability to produce greater varieties and numbers of fake goods, very few industries, if any, will remain beyond the reach of skilled and determined counterfeiters.

Typical Affected Products

Computer Software. This is the most affected of all products and industries touched by counterfeiting and piracy. In their Global Software Piracy Report, the Business Software Alliance (BSA) and the Software & Information Industry Association (SIIA) report findings that are disheartening but also encouraging.[21]

Music. The music industry is also heavily affected, reflecting the dark side of the digital revolution. In its Music Piracy Report of 2000, the International Federation of the Phonographic Industry (IFPI) reported that in 1999 the global pirated music market was estimated to have totaled 1.9 billion units. CD piracy increased to 500 million units, leaving music cassettes to account for 1.4 billion pirated units. The report notes that CD-recordable units made a significant impact.[22] The cost of this piracy was an estimated U.S. $4.1 billion. It is slightly less than in 1998, reflecting lower prices for illegal recordings and lower sales of illegal music cassettes. The report does note that world capacity for optical disk manufacturing rose 28 percent in 1999, and increased more than 340 percent over the prior five years. Internet piracy rose dramatically in 1999. While it is almost impossible to ascertain the exact number of illegal downloads via the Internet, Forrester Research estimated that there were more than one billion illegal downloads of music files in 1999.[23]

Films. The counterfeiting and piracy of films and other audiovisual productions occur in two basic forms: illegal diversion of cable and satellite delivery and physical copies, generally in the form of videocassettes. Focusing only on the sale of physical copies, the Motion Picture Association (MPA) estimated that worldwide video piracy costs American motion picture companies U.S. $2.5 billion a year in lost revenues.[24] The Organization for Economic Cooperation and Development (OECD), in its report Economic Impact of Counterfeiting, estimated that the video piracy rate for some countries can reach almost 100 percent.[25]

Luxury Goods and Fashion Wear. Counterfeit copies of luxury goods, especially fashion wear, proliferate, most notably in Europe where the major manufacturers are located. One common technique in this area is to import the fake clothing or items from one country, and to manufacture or import the labels from another. The fake labels are attached in the country of intended sale, thus making it much more difficult to identify fake goods in transit while these goods are in sufficiently large quantities to justify governmental enforcement action. One major source of these fakes are legitimate sub-contractor manufacturers, facilities which are legitimately authorized to manufacture original items, but who manufacture far in excess of the ordered amount, and sell the overruns out the back door at greatly reduced prices. Overruns create a sort of gray market, they are items illegitimately manufactured by a legitimate manufacturer, which are illegitimately sold or placed in the stream of commerce. Such overruns are essentially counterfeit goods which negatively affect the economy.[26]

Sportswear. The 1990s saw a huge upsurge in all things sports-related. Counterfeit sports wear is facilitated by several factors. The biggest segment of the market for these items is the youth market, the segment most willing to buy, even search out, counterfeit goods with well-known brand names at lower prices. The market for these items is also easily reachable, since, to a large extent, it centers around major events, particularly sport and music events. Mobile vendors of counterfeit goods are present in numbers at these events, and evidence suggests that these vendors are internationally organized and funded. Because they generally carry small inventories to these events, governmental authorities are restrained from putting a heavier emphasis on, or using more resources against them. Another factor which helps this area to prosper is that buyers mostly just want the brand name; counterfeiters can easily attach fake labels onto ordinary clothing, and thereby satisfy large numbers of the youth market.[27]

Perfumes. Perfume products are generally sold in established retail outlets, which lend price stability and authenticity to the market. However, the industry is experiencing attacks from counterfeiters and estimates that its losses in this area are greater than 5 percent of its total turnover. A willing public will generally purchase counterfeit perfumes from smaller shops and street vendors at so-called bargain prices where it is often claimed that the goods are stolen but are the real thing.

Toys. The toy industry can be divided into traditional toys and the rapidly growing electronic toy industry. Traditional toys are often copied and then sold under different names and trademarks, rendering infringement actions close to impossible. Electronic games are an ever more serious problem. Video games, such as those created for the handheld Nintendo best seller, the Gameboy,™ are copied and sold in huge numbers.[28]

Aircraft Components. Despite the fact that the legitimate market for aircraft parts is a heavily regulated industry, counterfeit aircraft parts slip into the chain of supply and distribution and can result in death and injury. The origin of counterfeit aircraft parts, where it can be ascertained, indicates that, with respect to accidents in the United States of America caused by such parts, more reported incidents involved parts produced in the United States of America than in other areas of the world.[29]

Automobile Components. This is an emerging growth area for counterfeiters, who target short-duration products, such as standard parts which are or can be sold off the shelf, or which can be fitted to different makes and models of automobiles. Such parts are less likely to carry any security device or anti-counterfeiting technology. The industry estimates its losses from counterfeit parts to be U.S. $12 billion per year, with the vast majority of that taking place in Europe.[30]

Pharmaceuticals. Because of the dramatic effects that counterfeit pharmaceuticals can have on public health and safety, including the death of unsuspecting victims, this is an area which currently receives more attention than ever before. The problem of counterfeit drugs and medicines is most acute in certain developing countries, where there might not exist a regulatory infrastructure to prevent or curb the problem. According to a recent OECD report on counterfeiting, the main factors underlying the problem of counterfeit pharmaceuticals in developing countries are "weak drug regulatory control and enforcement; scarcity and/or erratic supply of basic medicines; uncontrolled distribution chains; large price differentials between genuine and counterfeit medicines; lack of effective IPR protection; lack of regard for quality assurance; and corruption of the health care system."[31] It is estimated by the WHO that 6 percent of worldwide pharmaceutical sales are counterfeit, and that up to 70 percent of all medicine sold in some countries is counterfeit.[32]

Watches. It is estimated that 5 percent of global trade in watches is counterfeit. It is interesting to note that in some countries, such trade creates a barrier to the sale of legitimate products. The difficulties encountered by some governments in enforcing IPRs, and the public perception in some quarters that such counterfeiting is business as usual, all serve to hamper any efforts to beat back the illegal trade.[33]

Technological Advances and its Impact on Intellectual Property Law and Policy

Due to today's sophisticated global economy—with its easy and widespread access to technological advances such as computers, copiers and scanners—there are virtually no product lines, corporations, or consumers that can escape the reach of counterfeiters and/or pirates. IP is on its way to becoming the ultimate assets.[34] What has caused this transformation is the advent of the so-called knowledge economy supported by the Internet, which completely changed the coverage, amount, and speed of access to information (from which knowledge can be made).

Technological advances have made IP-type counterfeiting easier, as well, because most pirated audio, video, and software is accompanied by paper-based printed material (including any trademark), which is easily reproducible (both qualitatively and quantitatively) by modern printing techniques.[35] Ease of replication clearly present the most significant threat to the effectiveness and enforceability of copyright law. The advent of the compact disc clearly accelerated this phenomenon as it provided the pirate, or more accurately the criminal, with the ability to produce near perfect illegal recordings in the millions. And the recent development of cheap recordable optical discs has created another means of illegal mass duplication.

The Internet

The Internet has opened up vast new opportunities for both legitimate business and cybersmuggling crime. The card table pirate, who used to sell to dozens of customers at flea markets, now reaches millions through Internet auction sites and e-mail Spams. Counterfeiters, including organized criminal groups and terrorist organizations, have discovered that if you do not have to pay anyone for the research and development of those programs, selling them is a high margin and low risk proposition.[36]

Throughout the world, countries have begun to recognize the importance of the Internet as a vehicle for economic expansion. However, despite the promise that the Internet holds for innovative and creative industries, it also creates significant challenges, as it serves as an extremely efficient global distribution network for pirated products.[37]

Enforcement Measures. In order to realize the enormous potential of the Internet, a growing number of countries are implementing the World Intellectual Property Organization (WIPO) Internet Treaties and creating a legal environment conducive to investment and growth in Internet-related businesses and technologies.[38] An important first step in the fight against Internet piracy was achieved at the WIPO when it concluded two copyright treaties in 1996: the WIPO Copyright Treaty (WCT) and the WIPO Performances and Phonograms Treaty (WPPT), referred to as the WIPO Internet Treaties. These treaties help raise the minimum standards of IP protection around the world, particularly with respect to Internet-based delivery of copyrighted works. They clarify exclusive rights in the on-line environment and specifically prohibit the devices and services intended to circumvent technological protection measures for copyrighted works. Both treaties entered into force in 2002.

These treaties represent the consensus view of the world community that the vital framework of protection under existing agreements, including the Agreement on Trade Related Aspects of Intellectual

Property Rights (TRIPS), should be supplemented to eliminate any remaining gaps in copyright protection on the Internet that could impede the development of electronic commerce.

E-Commerce. E-commerce has already begun to have an extraordinary impact on the architecture of our markets and regulatory structures, and to raise issues that implicate different sectors of legal interest. As IP systems have been independently developed in different countries on the fundamental principle that each state has sovereignty over IP protection and enforcement within its territory, the international dimensions of e-commerce and the IP-related questions emerging from it complicate the development of solutions and caution against national interventions that would ignore potential cross-border impacts.

Cybersquatters. Another Internet-generated battle in the IP area is being fought over the eviction of cybersquatters who have taken over trademarks to which they have staked a claim in bad faith. Cybersquatters register domain names (essentially website addresses), which they have no intention of using and that are identical or similar to trademarks or famous names, and then try to sell them back to the holders of the mark or famous name at a profit. Cybersquatters, and some of the cases brought against them under the WIPO domain-name dispute resolution procedure, have received wide-spread coverage in the press, highlighting the importance of trademarks and their new manifestation as website identifiers, in the world of commerce. The domain name issue is yet another example of how the Internet has given a new dimension to a traditional form of IP, and has forced the IP community to find speedy and efficient solutions in order to resolve a problem of considerable economic importance.[39]

Intellectual Property Laws

Generally speaking, IP law aims at safeguarding creators and other producers of intellectual goods and services by granting them certain time-limited rights to control the use made of those productions. Those rights do not apply to the physical object in which the creation may be embodied but instead to the intellectual creation as such. As mentioned earlier, IP is traditionally divided into two branches, "industrial property" and "copyright." IPRs are protected by both domestic and international legal regimes.

Countries have laws to protect IP for two main reasons. One is to give statutory expression to the moral and economic rights of creators in their creations and the rights of the public in access to those creations. The second is to promote, as a deliberate act of Government policy, creativity and the dissemination and application of its results and to encourage fair trading which would contribute to economic and social development.

Paris Convention

In the field of industrial property, the immediate origin of an international regime can be found in the need for foreign inventors to be protected during the 1873 Vienna International Exposition. During the Vienna Congress (August 1873), associated with the Exposition, proposals were made to establish a system for the "legal protection of intellectual work." This was the basis for a series of Conferences in Paris in 1878, 1880, and, finally, in 1883, during which the first international Convention in the industrial property field was established. The Convention contains general principles of protection of industrial property (inventions, trademarks, industrial designs, appellations of origin, repression of unfair competition).

Berne Convention

In the field of literary and artistic works, the origin of the need for an international regime can be traced in a series of proposals formulated in a number of Congresses and Conferences in 1858, 1878, 1883, and 1884, which led to the Berne Conference of 1886 that adopted the first international copyright treaty. The Convention contains general principles of protection of literary and artistic works (e.g. novels, poems, plays, musical works, paintings, sculptures, etc.).

Conflicts of Laws

Because of the expansion of global activities that are involved with IPRs, an area which requires increased attention, from the perspective of international harmonization, is the body of disparate laws and legislation known as private international law. This body of law comes into play when civil litigation involves parties or courts in more than one country. With globalization of business and expanding technological development and telecommunications capacities, noticeably more international litigation is being pursued.

Litigants and their lawyers find that the laws of all Countries are not exactly the same, of course, even if they embody similar legal concepts. Consequently, the laws differ so much in some cases as to affect the outcome of litigation matters, depending in which country's courts the plaintiff decides to initiate the litigation. Because of this disparity in applicable laws, efforts are underway to further and more satisfactorily develop principles, so that the application of law in enforcement contexts will be fair and predictable. Issues such as jurisdiction, damages, and choice of applicable laws are at the heart of such initiatives.

Various trade agreements ensure the free flow and protection of IP among nations. The MPA encourages foreign governments to abide by, and fully implement, important agreements such as the Trade Related Aspects of Intellectual Property Rights (TRIPS) agreement of GATT, and the World Intellectual Property Organization (WIPO) treaties.

The European Initiatives

The European Community (EC) has taken action in the IP field mainly to harmonize existing national laws.[40] On October 15, 1998, the Commission presented a Green Paper[41] on the fight against counterfeiting and piracy in the Single Market in order to launch a debate on this subject with all interested parties. The areas of intervention suggested in the Green Paper related in particular to action by the private sector, the effectiveness of technical security provisions, penalties, and other means of ensuring compliance with IPRs, as well as administrative cooperation between the national authorities. Following the receipt of submissions, a public hearing in Munich on March 2 and 3, 1999, and a meeting of experts from the Member States on 3 November 1999, the European Parliament adopted a Regulation on this subject on May 4, 2000.[42] On November 30, 2000, the Commission presented a follow-up Communication to the Green Paper in which it indicated that it would be presenting a proposal for a Directive aimed at harmonizing the legislative, regulatory and administrative provisions of the Member States on the means of enforcing IPRs, and at ensuring that the rights available enjoy an equivalent level of protection in the Internal Market.[43] The proposal for a Directive on the enforcement of IPRs was generally welcomed by interested circles and was approved by the European Economic and Social Committee.[44] A proposal for a Directive on measures and procedures to ensure the enforcement of IPRs was issued on January 30, 2003.[45]

As the EC Green Paper entitled, *Combating Counterfeiting and Piracy in the Single Market* (1995), observed "Since the early 1950s counterfeiting and piracy have grown considerably to a point where they have now become a widespread phenomenon with a global impact." According to the EC Green Paper, the reasons for this phenomenon are various. They include developments in reprographic technologies, where digitization has facilitated the rapid and extensive production of copies at a minimal cost, the growth in world demand for branded items, as well as economic and political developments, such as the growth of international trade, the internationalization of the economy, the expansion of means of communication, and the opportunism of organized crime following the collapse of the political systems in central and eastern Europe and in the former Soviet Union.

Criminalization of Intellectual Property Violations in the United States

While owners of IP can protect their rights by pursuing civil remedies, the threat of civil sanctions often is insufficient to deter theft of trade secrets or infringement of trademarks, copyrights, or patents.[46,47] Indeed, some IP thieves view civil damages as simply another cost of doing business.[48]

The marked increase in IPC, combined with the lack of deterrence provided by civil remedies, has led the federal government (and most states) in the United States to enact criminal statutes to prevent the theft of IPRs.[49] The government has also begun a crackdown on trademark and copyright infringement.[50] The FBI's Operation "Counter Copy" and the DOJ's "Intellectual Property Rights Initiative"[51] are evidence of the government's commitment to prosecute IPC.[52]

Anti-piracy Laws in the United States

The Copyright Act of 1976 gave the United States some of the strongest anti-piracy legislation in the world. The Act was amended in 1982, substantially increasing the penalties for the illegal duplication of copyrighted material, making such offenses felonies on the first offense. The Sentencing Commission guidelines have reinforced these penalties. The Communications Act of 1984, and later amendments provide comparable penalties and remedies for cable TV and satellite pirates. Copyright owners may also file civil lawsuits against copyright infringers, and the government may file criminal charges. Online piracy is covered by the same laws that govern other forms of piracy. In addition, the United States government recently amended federal copyright statutes to specifically address Internet copyright issues and enhance the protection of IP online through the No Electronic Theft Act (NET Act) and the Digital Millennium Copyright Act (DMCA).

In addition, IP relations between the United States and most foreign countries are governed by an array of multilateral treaties and conventions as well as bilateral agreements, including the Universal Copyright Convention (UCC) and the Berne Convention.

Examples of Legislative Actions

Piracy Deterrence and Education Act of 2003. The "Piracy Deterrence and Education Act of 2003" orders the FBI to develop a deterrence program and facilitate information sharing among law enforcement agencies, Internet service providers and copyright owners of information. The FBI and the Recording Industry Association of America drafted a Memorandum of Understanding regarding the FBI Intellectual Property Rights Warning Program, which allows for the Recording Industry's use of the FBI seal in the same way that it has been used as a warning on videotapes, DVDs and movies for years.[53]

Database Protection. Copyright law currently provides little protection for databases.[54] The 106th Congress (1999-2000) saw an effort to correct this with the introduction of two database protection bills:[55] the Collections of Information Antipiracy Act ("CIAA") and the Consumer and Investors Access to Information Act of 1999.[56]

The Digital Millennium Copyright Act ("DMCA"). The DMCA Act became law in October 1998.[57] The DMCA provides liability limitations for transmitting online copyrighted material,[58] and it provides criminal penalties for circumvention of copyright protection systems[59] and for compromising the integrity of copyright management information.[60]

The No Electronic Theft Act ("NET Act"). The NET Act was enacted in December 1997.[61] This Act modified criminal copyright statutes by removing the financial requirement and making illegal reproduction or distribution of copyrighted materials a federal crime.[62] The No Electronic Theft Act was enacted in 1997 to reflect the fact that significant copyrighted infringement occurs not for financial gain but to harm the copyright owner or simply for personal gratification.[63] NET removed the requirement of financial gain.[64]

The Economic Espionage Act of 1996. The Economic Espionage Act ("EEA") of 1996 is a federal criminal statute dealing directly with the theft of commercial trade secrets.[65] It is the first federal statute that criminalizes private sector trade secret theft.

Trade Secrets Act. Prior to the EEA, the only federal statute that specifically addressed theft of trade secrets was the Trade Secrets Act ("TSA"), which criminalizes the unauthorized disclosure of confidential information to government employees.[66] However, because the TSA does apply to private sector employees[67] and only provides for misdemeanor sanctions,[68] federal prosecutors have preferred to rely on the National Stolen Property Act, the Mail and Wire Fraud Statutes to pursue charges of criminal trade secret misappropriation.[69]

National Stolen Property Act. The National Stolen Property Act ("NSPA")[70] provides criminal sanctions[71] for any person who "transports, transmits, or transfers in interstate or foreign commerce any goods, wares, merchandise, securities or money, of the value of $5,000 or more, knowing the same to have been stolen, converted or taken by fraud."[72,73] Federal courts have held that, under certain circumstances, the NSPA can apply to the theft of tangible property containing trade secrets,[74] even though the NSPA was not designed or intended to apply to trade secret theft.[75]

Mail and Wire Fraud Statutes. The mail and wire fraud statutes[76] provide criminal sanctions for using or attempting to use the mails[77] and wire services to perpetrate fraud.[78] Unlike the NSPA, these statutes may be applied to theft of intangible rights, such as trade secrets.[79] By imposing criminal penalties on those who use the mails or wires to defraud copyright owners, mail and wire fraud statutes can be used, where appropriate, to prosecute infringers.[80]

Racketeer Influenced and Corrupt Organizations Act. Criminal sanctions for theft of trade secrets are also available under RICO.[81] Although many cases brought under RICO are civil actions,[82] the predicate acts necessary to sustain a RICO claim are violations of criminal law.[83] Consequently, the elements of a civil and criminal RICO action are similar. The definition of racketeering activity applicable to the theft of trade secrets includes mail fraud,[84] wire fraud,[85] activity prohibited by the NSPA,[86] and the receipt of stolen property.[87]

Copyright Act. Criminal copyright infringement, first introduced into federal law in 1897, has traditionally been distinguished from civil violation by the requirement that the conduct be willful and undertaken for profit.[88] The criminal copyright statute has been amended frequently as Congress attempts to strengthen the Act and broaden its scope.[89]

Copyright Felony Act. Enacted in October 1992, the Copyright Felony Act[90] responded primarily to the growing problem of large-scale computer software piracy. For a little more than a century, criminal copyright infringement provisions have been a part of the federal copyright act and distinguished from civil remedies by the requirements of willfulness and profit-making desire.[91] In 1992, Congress enacted the Copyright Felony Act as a response to a software piracy.[92] Prior to that time, only the infringing copying of audiovisual works, motion pictures, and sound recordings was a violation of federal criminal law.[93] The Copyright Felony Act caused the protection, by criminal sanction, of all copyrighted works.[94]

The Communications Act. It is a violation of federal law (17 U.S.C. §106(1)) to distribute, rent or sell illegally duplicated copies, even if the copies are made by someone else (17 U.S.C. §106(3)). The Communications Act of 1934, as amended, (47 U.S.C. §605) and related statutes also prohibit the unauthorized reception of films via satellite or cable TV. Copyright infringement and violation of the Communications Act are felonies under federal law and carry maximum sentences of up to five years in jail and/or a $250,000 fine. Both laws also provide for copyright owners to seek civil damages.

Money Laundering Act. The money laundering statute, 18 U.S.C. §1956, defines money laundering, and includes the receipt of proceeds from trafficking in counterfeit goods or goods infringing on copyright as specified unlawful activities.[95]

State laws relating to video piracy are not copyright laws per se. However, various states have so-called "truth-in-labeling" laws and other statutes that can be effectively used to prosecute film and video pirates. Forty-five states have "True Name and Address" statutes which can be used to combat video piracy. These laws impose criminal penalties for the rental or sale of video cassettes that do not bear the true name and address of the manufacturer. Video pirates who fail to identify themselves as the "manufacturer" of illegally duplicated cassettes violate these statutes. In some states these laws are currently first offense misdemeanors.

Initiatives Toward Enforcement of Intellectual Property Rights

At the international level, a number of governments are reinforcing their legal framework and institutional arrangements to comply with the existing international treaties. Generally, enforcement of IPRs can take four basic forms:

- Administrative enforcement, such as seizure of infringing goods by a customs office;
- Criminal enforcement, in which the state, generally through the police, is the moving party in a criminal action against the infringer;
- Civil enforcement, in which the right holder, or someone in possession of valid rights, such as an assignee or licensee, takes prescribed legal action, such as in court by filing a civil action against an infringer, and perhaps seeking an injunction;
- Technological enforcement, in which producers of products and services employ technological means to protect IPRs against infringement (for example, encryption of digital copyright works).

These measures are limited to applicable laws (for example, in many countries, criminal enforcement is not applicable in the case of a patent infringement). Administrative measures and civil measures are linked in some countries. For some states, it is hard to determine the extent to which the state should use public resources to help enforce a private party's right. However, effective enforcement has become an international obligation under the TRIPS Agreement, as it is vital in promoting trade and fostering fair competition in market-oriented economies. Advantages and disadvantages are shown below.

The issue of the enforcement of IPRs cuts across many segments and layers of society; it affects them all in varying degrees and in different ways. Counterfeiting and piracy constitute the bulk of the problem. Because of the various effects on society, there are numerous organizations such as the World Customs Organization (WCO)[96] and INTERPOL involved in protection of IPRs as well as several noteworthy law enforcement initiatives.[97,98] There are other international organizations that have shaped the course of IPR protection. For example, in the wake of World War II, the World Bank and the International Monetary Fund (IMF) collaborated to create the General Agreement on Tariffs and Trade (GATT).[99] GATT was established to provide a framework for a multilateral economic system. In order to promote that objective, it sponsored "rounds" as a forum for signatory nations to meet and further the established goals of the organization.[100]

The United States and other developed countries view the GATT as the appropriate forum in which to strengthen IPRs.[101] Under GATT, the United States and other developed countries were able to set high international standards for the protection of IP with those standards being enforced under the World Trade Organization (WTO).[102,103] The United States has also included provisions protecting IPRs in multinational documents. For instance, the United States insisted that NAFTA contain a provision on IP protection in an effort to combat piracy in Mexico.[104]

World Trade Organization

In 1994, at the "Uruguay Round," the World Trade Organization (WTO) was created and replaced GATT's old administrative structure.[105] The WTO is the only global international organization dealing with the rules of trade between nations with the goal of helping producers conduct their business.[106] The WTO structure is made up of three primary pillars: The Agreement on Trade Related Aspects of Intellectual Property Rights (TRIPS),[107] the General Agreement on Trade in Services (GATS), and GATT—1994.[108] The TRIPS Agreement has been haled as "a landmark in the evolution of an international consensus on IP protection and is the most significant advance in the international protection of IP since the adoption of the Berne and Paris Conventions in the late nineteenth century."[109]

The Agreement on Trade Related Aspects of Intellectual Property Rights

The TRIPS Agreement is based on the principles of national treatment and most favored nation (MFN) status. National treatment under TRIPS provides that "each Member shall accord to the nationals of other Members treatment no less favorable than that it accords to its own nationals with regard to the protection of IP..."[110] This provision is similar to the protection afforded by the Berne and Paris Conventions. MFN, on the other hand, requires that in IPR protection, any advantage, favor, privilege or immunity granted by one member nation to the nationals of any, other country shall be conferred immediately, and unconditionally, to the nationals of all other member nations.[111] Thus, MFN supports national treatment by assuring that all MFN nations are treated equally.

These international, multilateral agreements signal a fundamental shift in the global protection of IPRs. The level of international cooperation and commitment to these organizations is unprecedented in the history of IPRs.

Although the United States and other WICs strongly favor worldwide enforcement of IPRs, much of the Third World opposes such enforcement.[112] The United States position of strengthening international IP enforcement is based on at least two motives: 1) the economic benefits to the United States which enhanced enforcement of IP could yield;[113] and 2) a belief that improved protection of IP is essential for the economic development of all countries.[114] Some Third World countries, however, view WICs' attempts to enforce IP as a continuation of colonialist policies in which WICs control the economic structure of the lesser-developed nations by allocating technology and extracting exorbitant royalties in return.[115] In addition, many developing countries believe that WICs have an obligation to aid the development of poorer countries rather than retarding their growth through restrictive IP policies.[116]

Intellectual Property Crimes are Perceived as Victimless Crimes

Intellectual property crime (IPC) is well established and few people will argue that it is not at least a $400 to $450 billion a year crime problem. One would think that this fact in itself would make prosecution of this crime a high priority for law enforcement around the world. Considering that in the United States alone IPC represents a $200 to $250 billion dollar loss, any problem of this magnitude should draw the attention of law enforcement at both national and international levels. The question still remains unanswered as to why this has not always been a high priority crime area for law enforcement.[117] Both individuals and businesses have an interest in protecting the investments made in various forms of IP. There is a great deal to be lost when IPR are not protected.

IP piracy is unfortunately considered as a low-risk, high-profit criminal enterprise that is widely tolerated.[118] It is common for the public to think of IP piracy as a victimless crime, a minor economic offense that only affects wealthy corporations and does no real harm to society or to individuals. Such activities are frequently a low priority for domestic and international law enforcement agencies as well. Counterfeiters are counting on law enforcement, prosecutors and the courts to take a soft approach toward those who engage in what appears to be victimless counterfeiting. Until investigations of these crimes prove otherwise, the extent of the threat arising from these activities is unknown. Those involved in trafficking counterfeit goods are everywhere and, despite the perception that product counterfeiting is harmless and victimless, consumers, companies and governments are all victims.[119] The cross-industry impact of the crime dilutes its importance on any one industry. It is a crime that crosses national borders, so it is difficult to investigate from end to end. The distribution network is very dispersed, often ending up with poor immigrants standing on street corners with items that seem too good to resist. The penalty, if arrested and convicted, for engaging in this kind of activity is also low, therefore the deterrence impact is not great.[120]

Law enforcement and prosecutors get little credit for arrests and/or for seizures. It's often viewed as a civil enforcement problem and often time the question becomes why not let the wealthy companies or the wealthy industries police this problem themselves? Consumers believe that the companies involved make so much money already, why—and how are they going to be hurt if the consumers buy a disc, a CD or a designer product? From the consumers' perspective, the profits of designer goods companies and drug companies are already high, profits of certain sports retailers—producers also seem to be high. Therefore, the connection between the consumers' act, the consumers' purchase, and the crime seems to be far. Furthermore, the victim is not anyone that the consumer knows or can identify with in terms of a human face.[121]

United States efforts have contributed to strengthened intellectual property legislation overseas, but enforcement in many countries remains weak. Further, United States efforts face significant challenges.

Law Enforcement Challenges

Law enforcement agencies have to recognize that Intellectual Property Crime is not a victimless crime. Law enforcement does not always investigate IPC cases. Investigations when initiated often tend to be seizure-based and do not extend to following onward flows of money. Even if law enforcement were to follow onward flows of money, given the high level of cash-based transactions involved, it is difficult to establish with any precision the end destination of the financial flows.

What Needs to Be Done

One question is whether the incentives for introducing a Western-style IP system should be given to all countries or only to countries that play a dominate role in IPR's violations. In other words, should the countries be ignored until they reach the stage-two to stage-three transition or should the incentives to implement an IP system be introduced even in stage-one countries?

A uniform policy of encouraging all countries to adopt IP protection is probably preferable.[122] It should be easier to encourage a developing country to adopt an IP system before it reaches the "pirating" stage of economic development. Once a country has developed a significant number of businesses that profit from pirating, these businesses will become a political force that will oppose the adoption of IP regulations. In addition, the United States might find it extremely difficult to determine when a country has reached the proper developmental stage for the imposition of an IP system. It would be simpler to encourage an IP system in all countries regardless of developmental stage.[123] The incentives should continue until the country has reached a level of development where benefits of IP protection clearly outweigh its costs.[124]

Even though IP protection is important for developing nations, most have failed to provide IP adequate protection, and this failure has facilitated the rampant piracy of goods.[125] The challenges of IPRs protection have become correspondingly global, with concerted action at the national, regional and international levels. The reasons underlying such disrespect for IPRs are many and varied, and range from greed, perceived necessity, lack of awareness, and ruthless criminal intent, all the way to innocent mistake. The scale of such disrespect also varies considerably, from copying a protected work in one's home to large-scale commercial criminal enterprises that produce hundreds of thousands of illegal copies. When illegal products take market share (or even kill a potential market), and when recouping an investment is prevented by intervening criminal activity, enforcement mechanisms are called into play to protect vital interests, not only of the players and entities mentioned, but also those of the public.

Recent Efforts Toward Protection of Intellectual Property Rights

Senior officials from government, law enforcement and the business sector, met at the First Global Congress on Combating Counterfeiting in May 2004 in Brussels, Belgium. The Congress called for concrete action in curbing the growing problem of counterfeiting, which they estimated to be worth EUR 500 billion annually, equivalent to more than seven percent of global trade. More than 300 delegates attended the conference co-sponsored by the World Customs Organization and Interpol, with the support of the World Intellectual Property Organization. The purpose of the Congress was to develop a collective understanding of the extent of the counterfeit and piracy problem, identify effective measures of governments and the private sector in anti-counterfeiting and anti-piracy work, generate ideas for further cooperation and begin to identify solutions that will make a real difference in the coming decade.[126]

The Congress recommended action in four main areas:

- Substantially increased cooperation and communication among all stakeholders.
- Better enforcement and stiffer penalties to deter counterfeiting.
- Extended training and resources for law enforcement.
- Increased public awareness of the full impact and costs of counterfeiting.[127]

According to this Congress, any future discussions should be focused on the following topics:

- Developing a consensus on the full dimensions and related costs of counterfeiting to consumers, governments and industry.
- Developing common understandings of the prevailing attitudes of governments, the private sector and consumers towards counterfeiting.
- Generating common understanding of what is being done and what more needs to be done in the fight against counterfeiting.
- Examining and understanding current international instruments for cooperation among governments in enforcement work, and identifying enhancements required for strengthening enforcement efforts.

Possible Solutions for Intellectual Property Crimes

In order to combat counterfeiting and piracy effectively, the following measures can be implemented: a) monitoring by the private sector; b) the use of technical devices; c) sanctions and other means of enforcing IPRs; and d) administrative cooperation among the competent authorities.[128]

Monitoring by the Private Sector

Most monitoring can be carried out privately by national or international professional associations or organizations, such as manufacturers' associations, trade mark proprietors' associations and collecting societies. It generally consists of observing market trends, advising and supporting the industries concerned, collaborating with the authorities (customs, police, the courts, etc.), monitoring suspicious activities and detecting acts of counterfeiting and piracy, keeping the public informed and, where necessary, convincing the government of the need to amend or revise the existing laws.[129]

The Use of Technical Devices

One of the means of combating counterfeiting and piracy at the disposal of the holders of IPRs is the use of technical devices to protect and authenticate their products or services. Technical devices may take many forms: security holograms, optical devices, chip cards, magnetic systems, biometric codes, special inks, microscopic labels, etc. These technical devices facilitate the prosecution and punishment of counterfeiting and piracy. Through them, unlawful uses of works, products or services can easily be traced back to the source, so that infringers can be identified and prosecuted more effectively. However, although technical devices act as a filter for the most obvious counterfeit or pirated goods, they do not ordinarily defeat the most highly organized infringers, who succeed in turn in reproducing the devices. Such devices must, therefore, enjoy suitable legal protection to prevent them from being infringed, manipulated or neutralized.[130]

Sanctions and Other Means of Enforcing Intellectual Property Rights

As previously mentioned, the TRIPS Agreement obliges all Member countries to implement the enforcement mechanisms contained in that Agreement. This includes both criminal and civil remedies. All Member States provide by law that counterfeiters and pirates are in principle liable to criminal penalties, but the level and severity of the penalties vary considerably from one Member State to another. For violation of certain types of right, no criminal penalty is provided. Some Member States have, however, been tightening up the criminal law in respect of counterfeiting and piracy in recent years.

Failure to comply with an injunction is punishable by specific penalties, usually a fine payable either to the State or to the person seeking the injunction. The infringer may be required to pay damages to the rightful holder to make good the loss or damage caused by the infringement of the intellectual property right.

Other measures for combating counterfeiting and piracy, include the sanction of publicity, through the publication of judgments, orders to reveal information about the origin of the goods, the distribution channels and the identity of any third parties involved in the production and distribution of the goods.

Future Policy Considerations for Protection of Intellectual Property Rights

A number of future policy considerations are evident at this time. Some of them are listed here.

1. There is a need to allocate resources to the investigation of IPC and to trace its financial flows.
2. Successful models for investigating IPC nationally and internationally should be established. Various agencies involved in intellectual property crime investigation must help to coordinate international action against intellectual property crime. The models should be based on professional law enforcement and intelligence agency investigations into organized crime and terrorist group involvement in intellectual property crime and other forms of criminality.
3. An intellectual property crime action group should be established by including a wide range of stakeholders from customs, police and private industry.
4. Encouragement should been given to Federal law enforcement agencies to cooperatively pursue investigations of counterfeiting and to root out and prosecute manufacturers, distributors and other involved in the trafficking of counterfeit goods. The exchange of information and intelligence gathering must be enhanced among law enforcement agencies worldwide. Strategies and programs to combat international criminal activity linked to IP infringement must be developed.
5. The operational contact network of private and public partners throughout the world must be enhanced and strengthened. International cross-border multi-agency investigations into intellectual property crime must be coordinated.
6. Awareness of intellectual property crime must be raised with the general public.
7. Data and reporting of intellectual property crime must improve.
8. New IP laws are needed to address IPC.

9. Increase the level of vigilance at the border regardless of the products involved. Counterfeiting and piracy impact national economic security.
10. Ensure that legislation permits ex officio border and criminal enforcement, including prosecution.
11. There is a need for legislation to detain, seize, forfeit and destroy pirate/counterfeit goods being imported, exported and moving in-transit, as well as seizure and destruction of equipment used to produce such goods.
12. Raise the stakes for the individuals involved in IP theft. The federal criminal statute against trafficking in counterfeit goods should be strengthened. There is a need for sentencing guidelines that require more stringent penalties (fines/imprisonment).
13. Examine the extent to which organized crime is involved in the international trade of counterfeit and pirated products.
14. There is a need for cooperation among law enforcement agencies and the high-tech industry.
15. Finally, more research and publications sre needed on this topic.

Future Research Issues

The topic of IP violations is a complicated and challenging topic to research and analyze. The following unanswered questions on this topic provide a starting point for future research that aims to provide practical solutions to policy makers, legislatures, government agencies, private industry and IPR holders around the world who are grappling with protection of IPRs.

- What is the status of international investigations into the problem of IP violations?
- Where does this criminal activity appear most prevalent?
- Which governments are most aggressively tackling this issue?
- Which governments are failing to address the problem?
- What are effective law enforcement strategies to combat IPC?
- What legislative responses, if any, would be appropriate?
- What international cooperative efforts should be explored?
- What is the most effective means by which to educate consumers about this growing problem?[131]

Each of these questions represents a research topic unto itself.

Whether, and to what extent, society realizes the full value of IPRs in the new economy and in modern society irrefutably impacts on economic, social, and cultural development. In addition to political will and the implementation of national legislation compliant with all the relevant treaties of IPRs enforcement, government leaders may wish to consider the importance of fostering an IP culture.

Appreciating the value of IPRs and the potential positive impact they can have on society, will raise awareness in all persons involved or touched by the process. In the IP culture, government officials and agencies act to increase value and raise standards of living by advocating an increased appreciation of IPRs. The private sector, from multinational corporations down to SMEs, recognizes the value of IPRs in knowledge-based industries and economies. The public also must understand the benefits of purchasing legitimate goods and services.

Given that we are all aware of the counterfeit goods sold in flea markets and on the streets of major cities, the added knowledge that counterfeiters have moved into auto parts, medicines, home appliances and electrical goods should give us pause to start thinking of the counterfeiting problem as a frontal attack on consumer safety and economic stability. Because no industry sector is immune from attack by counterfeiters and no country is exempt from this type of criminal activity, both corporate and governmental law enforcement resources must be committed to combating IP crime.

Today's level of counterfeiting has reached the point that it now requires government intervention to confront the organized crime elements that are involved around the world. Industry is neither equipped to deal with organized crime nor is it a function for industry to pursue this type of criminal activity. Because of a reluctance to combat product counterfeiting in the past, it is now being seen as a real and dangerous threat to consumers and industry. The proliferation of this problem requires governments to take steps in the domestic market, at the border, as well as in free trade zones that seem to be lawless territory.

Notes

1.   Nasheri, H. 2005. *Economic Espionage and Industrial Spying*. Cambridge University Press: New York and London.
2.   The research for this article was made possible, in part, by a grant from the International Center at the National Institute of Justice on intellectual property as part of its research agenda on transnational crime, and through a Research Fellowship at the Institute of Advanced Legal Studies (IALS) at the University of London. Special thanks go to the staff at the IALS Library at the University of London for providing assistance with research materials. However, any opinions, findings and conclusions, or recommendations expressed in this article are those of the author and do not necessarily reflect the views of any government officials o granting entities.
3.   The Convention Establishing the World Intellectual Property Organization in Stockholm on July 14, 1967, (Article 2(viii)). Last retrieved February 3, 2005, from http://www.wipo.int/treaties/en/convention/ rtdocs_wo029.html

4. Powell, R. & Rohan, P. (1996). *Powell on real property.* New York: Matthew Bender.

5. Chisum, D.S. (1997). Chisum on patents: A treatise on the law of patentability, validity and infringement. New York: Matthew Bender.

6. World Intellectual Property Organization. *About intellectual property.* Retrieved February 28, 2004 from, http://www.wipo.org/about-ip/en/.

7. Ibid.

8. Ibid.

9. Its origin dates back to ancient times, when craftsmen reproduced their signatures, or marks, on their artistic or utilitarian products. Over the years, the practice of using these marks evolved into today's system of trademark registration and protection.

10. The creator—or the owner of the copyright in a work—can enforce rights in the courts where the owner may obtain an order to stop unauthorized use (often called piracy), as well as obtain damages for loss of financial rewards and recognition.

11. New Patent System Boosts Intellectual Property Rights. (2001, September 3). *Business World,* p. 30.

12. Hyde, Henry J. Opening Remarks before the Committee on International Relations; *Intellectual property crimes: Are proceeds from counterfeited goods funding terrorism?* (16 July 2003). Retrieved February 2004 from, www.fnsg.com.

13. Ibid.

14. Piracy is "the unauthorized and illegal reproduction or distribution of materials protected by copyright, patent, or trademark law." Garner, Bryan A. (Ed.) (1999). *Black's Law Dictionary* (7th ed. 1169). : West Group.

15. To counterfeit is "to forge, copy, or imitate (something) without a right to do so and with the purpose of deceiving or defrauding." Garner, Bryan A. (Ed.) (1999). *Black's Law Dictionary* (7th ed. 1169). : West Group.

16. In July 2003, the House Committee on International Relations held a hearing entitled "Intellectual Property Crimes: Are Proceeds From Counterfeited Goods Funding Terrorism?" The Secretary General of Interpol testified at this hearing.

17. There are various loss estimates due to counterfeiting and piracy. For example, the International Intellectual Property Association estimated that losses due to piracy of U.S. copyrighted materials around the world have reached $20 to $22 billion annually (not including Internet piracy). According to the 2003 Department of Homeland Security statistics on seizures, the majority of goods seized at U.S. ports of entry were counterfeit goods, worth more than $90 million.

18. Interviews conducted by author with David Mahon, Supervisory Special Agent, Cyber Crime Squad, Federal Bureau of Investigation—Denver Division, 2004.

19. Interviews conducted by author with David Mahon, Supervisory Special Agent, Cyber Crime Squad, Federal Bureau of Investigation—Denver Division, 2004.

20. Office of the United States Trade Representative. (2004). *USTR - Intellectual property: 2004 special 301 report.* Washington, DC.

21. Business Software Alliance and Software & Information Industry Association (2003). *Global Software Piracy Report.* (Issue 3). BSA Global Software Privacy Study, published in 2003, and located at <http://global.bsa.org/global-study/2003_GSPS.pdf>. BSA "Global Software Piracy Report" in 2000, located at <http://global.bsa.org/usa/globallib/piracy/piracystats99.phtml?CFID=14731&CFTOKEN=33412057>. BSA is located in Washington, DC.

22. International Federation of the Phonographic Industry. (2000). Music piracy report 2000 (Issue 2). London: International Federation of the Phonographic Industry.

23. Ibid.

24.   Ibid.
25.   Organization for Economic Co-operation and Development. (1998). Economic impact of counterfeiting (Issue 12). Pans: Paris; Washington, DC: Organization for Economic Co-operation and Development.
26.   Organization for Economic Co-operation and Development. (1998). Economic impact of counterfeiting (Issue 13). Pans: Paris; Washington, DC: Organization for Economic Co-operation and Development.
27.   Organization for Economic Co-operation and Development. (1998). Economic impact of counterfeiting (Issue 14). Pans: Paris; Washington, DC: Organization for Economic Co-operation and Development.
28.   Organization for Economic Co-operation and Development. (1998). Economic impact of counterfeiting (Issue 15). Pans: Paris; Washington, DC: Organization for Economic Co-operation and Development.
29.   Organization for Economic Co-operation and Development. (1998). Economic impact of counterfeiting (Issue 16). Pans: Paris; Washington, DC: Organization for Economic Co-operation and Development.
30.   Organization for Economic Co-operation and Development. (1998). Economic impact of counterfeiting (Issue 17). Pans: Paris; Washington, DC: Organization for Economic Co-operation and Development.
31.   Organization for Economic Co-operation and Development. (1998). Economic impact of counterfeiting (Issue 18). Pans: Paris; Washington, DC: Organization for Economic Co-operation and Development.
32.   Organization for Economic Co-operation and Development. (1998). Economic impact of counterfeiting (Issue 18). Pans: Paris; Washington, DC: Organization for Economic Co-operation and Development.
33.   Organization for Economic Co-operation and Development. (1998). Economic impact of counterfeiting (Issue 9). Pans: Paris; Washington, DC: Organization for Economic Co-operation and Development.
34.   *Aurigin Systems.* (1999). In K.G. Rivette and D. Kline, *Rembrandts in the attic: Unlocking the hidden value of patents.* Cambridge, MA: Harvard Business School Press.
35.   Friedman, D. (1994). Standards as intellectual property: An economic approach. *University of Dayton Law Review,* 19, 1109-1117.
36.   Fighting Cybercrime: Hearing before the Subcommittee on Crime of the Committee on Judiciary, House of Representatives. 107th Cong., 1st Sess. (2001). Last retrieved February 3, 2005, from http://judiciary.house.gov/ legacy/72616.pdf.
37.   Office of the United States Trade Representative. (*2004*). *USTR - Intellectual property: 2004 special 301 report.* Washington, DC.
38.   Ibid.
39.   Interviews conducted by author with Edwin Kwakwa, Legal Counsel, World Intellectual Property Organization, Geneva, Switzerland, (2004). World Intellectual Property Organization. (2004, March). WIPO, Information technology and internet domain name disputes. Cleveland: Case Western Reserve University School of Law, Center for Law, Technology and the Arts: Edwind Kwakwa.
40.   Eg trade marks (First Council Directive 89/104/EEC of 21 December 1988 to approximate the laws of the Member States relating to trade marks, OJ L 40, 11.2.1989, p. 1.8), designs (Directive 98/71/EC of the European Parliament and of the Council of 13 October 1998 on the legal protection of designs, OJ L 289, 28.10.1998, p. 28), patents for biotechnological inventions (Directive 99.44.EC of the European Parliament and of the Council of 6 July 1998 on the legal protection of biotechnological inventions, OJ L 213, 30.7.1998, p. 13), aspects of copyright

and related rights (Council Directive 91/250/EEC of 14 May 1991 on the legal protection of computer programs, OJ L 122, 17.5.1991, p. 42; Council Directive 92/100/EEC of 19 November 1992 on rental right and lending right and on certain rights related to copyright in the field of intellectual property, OJ L 346, 27.11.1992, p. 61; Council Directive 93/83/EEC of 27 September 1993 on the coordination of certain rules concerning copyright and rights related to copyright applicable to satellite broadcasting and cable retransmission, OJ L 248, 6.10.1993, p. 15; Council Directive 93/98/EEC of 29 October 1993 harmonizing the term of protection of copyright and certain related rights, OJ L 290, 24.11.1993, p. 9; Directive 96/9/EC of the European Parliament and of the Council of 11 March 1996 on the legal protection of databases, OJ L 77, 27.3.1996, P. 20; Directive 2001/29/EC of the European Parliament and of the Council of 22 May 2001 on the harmonization of certain aspects of copyright and related rights in the information society, OJ L 167, 22.6.2001, p. 10..) resale right for the benefit of the authors of original works of art (Directive 2001/84/EC of the European Parliament and of the Council of 27 September 2001 on resale rights for the benefit of the authors of original works of art, OJ L 272, 13.10.2001, p. 32) and the Directive on the harmonization of certain aspects of copyright and related rights in the information society 13.

41.   COM(98) 569 Final.

42.   OJC C 41, 7.2.2001, p. 56.

43.   COM (2000) 789 Final.

44.   OJ C 221, 7.8.2001, p. 20.

45.   COM (2003) 46 Final.

46.   Historically, civil remedies for theft of trade secrets have been sought in litigation. However, because increased technological complexity, delays in civil litigation, and advances in computer technology have allowed thieves to profit more rapidly from trade secrets, traditional remedies of injunctions and civil damages have become largely ineffective. Furthermore, because of the intangible nature of trade secrets and the fact that thieves are often judgment-proof or too sophisticated to be pursued, civil remedies are frequently illusory.

47.   Mason, J.D., Mossinghoff, G., and Oblon, D. (1999). The Economic Espionage Act: Federal protection for corporate trade secrets. *Computer Law*, 16, 14-15.

48.   Carr C., Morton, J. and Furniss, J. (2000). The Economic Espionage Act: Bear trap or mousetrap? *Texas Intellectual Property Law Journal* 8, 159-167.

49.   Interview conducted by author with Wolfgang Starein, Director, World Intellectual Property Organization, Geneva, Switzerland, (2004). United States Department of Justice Criminal Division. *Prosecuting Intellectual Property Crimes Manual, Introduction.* Retrieved February 2004 from, http://www.cybercrime. gov/ipmanual/intro.htm. ("As the modern economy grows increasingly reliant on intellectual property, the proliferation of computers and computer networks has made the illegal reproduction and distribution of protected material much easier to accomplish.").

50.   United States Dep't of Justice. (Press Release). (1997). FBI releases first results of nationwide crackdown on criminal trademark and copyright fraud. Retrieved December 10, 2002 from, http://www.usdoj.gov/criminallcybercrimefl95_ag.htm (presenting results of Operation "Counter Copy" enforcement effort against copyright and trademark violations).

51.   Green, J.T. (2001). Don't steal this article: Using the criminal provisions of the Copyright Act, 4 *Business Crimes Bulletin* 3 (2001) (noting this initiative quickly netted four guilty pleas for copyright infringement by college students).

52. United States Department of Justice Criminal Division. *Prosecuting Intellectual Property Crimes Manual, Introduction.* Retrieved February 2004 from, http://www.cybercrime. gov/ipmanual/intro.htm.

53. Monroe, Jana D. Federal Document Clearing House Congressional Testimony. *Copyright Enforcement and Internet Copyright Issues*, (17 July 2003). Retrieved February 3,2005, from http://judiciary.house.gov/ HearingTestimony. aspx?ID=130.

54. See *Feist Publications, Inc. v. Rural Telephone Serv. Co.*, 499 US. 340, 349, 353 (1991) (holding originality, not sweat of brow—hard work in compiling facts—to be key to copyrightability).

55. Tomlin, D. H. (2001). Sui generis database protection: Cold comfort for hot news. 19 *Comm. Lawyer* 15, 16, 18.

56. H.R. 1858, 106th Cong. (1999). This bill was introduced by United States Representative Thomas Bliley (R-VA). See John J. Cotter et al., Using and Misusing Third Party Resources, 661 PLI/Pat 213 (2001), at 254. H.R. 1858 prevented the distribution of a duplicate of another's database in direct competition with the original database.

57. Pub. L. No. 105-304, 112 Stat. 2877 (codified as amended at 17 U.S.C. § 512 (1998)). See *United States v. Elcom Ltd.*, 203 F. Supp. 2d 1111, 1127-1129 (N.D. CaL 2002) (upholding DCMA to constitutional challenge); see also Goldstone, D. and O'Leary, M. (2001). Novel criminal copyright infringement issues related to the Internet. Retrieved January 21, 2003 from, http://www.cybercrime. gov/usamay2001_5.htm. (discussing enactment of the DMCA).

58. 17 U.S.C. § 512 (2000).

59. 17 U.S.C. § 1201 (2000).

60. 17 U.S.C. § 1202 (2000).

61. No Electronic Theft (NET) Act of 1997, Pub. L. No. 105-147, 111 Stat. 2678 (1997).

62. Coblenz, M. (1999). Intellectual Property Crimes. *Albany Law Journal of Science and Technology*, 9, 235-244. (commenting on history of criminal copyright statutes). The NET Act is the centerpiece of DOJ efforts to combat intellectual property infringement, especially in the New York-New Jersey area, California, Massachusetts and the Southern District of Florida. Eric H. Holder, Jr. (Press Conference). (1999). Announcing the Intellectual Property Rights Initiative. Retrieved January 21, 2003 from, http://www.usdoj.gov/criminal/cybercrime/ dagipini.htm. (detailing new interdepartmental commitment).

63. Hsieh, L., McCarthy, J. and Monkus, E. (1998). Intellectual Property Crimes. *American Criminal Law Review* 35, 899-915. "A college student pleaded guilty to illegally distributing movies, music and software programs [through] his Web site in what federal prosecutors...said was the first Internet piracy conviction under a 1997 law." Students pleads guilty to software pirating. (1999, August 21). *Houston Chronicle*, p. 2C.

64. Hsieh, L., McCarthy, J. and Monkus, E. Intellectual Property Crimes, *American Criminal Law Review*, 35, 899-915.

65. Computer Crime and Intellectual Property Section. Chapter VIII: Theft of Commercial Trade Secrets (2000). Last retrieved February 3, 2005, from http://www. cybercrime.gov/ipmanual/O8ipma.htm.

66. 18 U.S.C. § 1905 (2000) (describing crime of disclosure of confidential information by an officer or employee of the United States); see *United States v. Wallington*, 889 F.2d 573, 577-78 (5th Cir. 1989) (noting Act prohibits disclosure of information only if information is confidential and federal employee knew information to be so).

67.   18 U.S.C. § 1905 (2000) (limiting scope to "an officer or employee of the United States or of any department or agency thereof, any person acting on behalf of the Office of Federal Housing Enterprise Oversight, or agent of the Department of Justice as defined in the Antitrust Civil Process Act").

68.   18 U.S.C. § 1905 (2000) (providing for fine or imprisonment of not more than one year, or both, removal from office or employment, for disclosure of confidential information by officer or employee of United States). Pooley, J.H.A. (1996). Understanding the Economic Espionage Act of 1996. *Texas Intellectual Property Law Journal, 5,* 177-180.

69.   Pooley, J.H.A. (1996). Understanding the Economic Espionage Act of 1996. *Texas Intellectual Property Law Journal, 5,* 177-180.

70.   18 U.S.C. § 2314 (2000). The NSPA was intended "to fight the 'roving criminal' whose access to automobiles made it easy to move stolen property across state lines...frustrating local law enforcement." Krakaur, K.D. & Juman, R.C. (1997). Two New Federal Offenses Help Battle Corporate Espionage. *Business Crimes Bulletin: Compliance & Litigation,* 4, 7. See Pooley, supra note 26, at 179-180 (indicating 18 U.S.C. §§ 2314, 2315 are also known as the Interstate Transportation of Stolen Property Act ("ITSP")).

71.   18 U.S.C. § 2314 (2000) (levying sanctions in form of fine and/or imprisonment for up to ten years).

72.   Section 2314 imposes criminal sanctions on any person who: having devised or intending to devise any scheme or artifice to defraud, or for obtaining money or property by means of false or fraudulent pretenses, representations, or promises, transports or causes to be transported, or induces any person or persons to travel in, or to be transported in interstate or foreign commerce in the execution or concealment of a scheme or artifice to defraud that person or those persons of money or property having a value of $5,000 or more.

73.   18 U.S.C. § 2314 (2000).

74.   See *United States v. Stegora,* 849 F.2d 291, 292 (8th Cir. 1988) (ruling theft of sample of synthetic casting material used in repairing broken bones falls under NSPA even though major portion of its value comes from intangible component); *United States v. Bottone,* 365 F.2d 389, 393-94 (2d Cir. 1966) (holding NSPA applicable to theft of copies of documents containing trade secrets); *United States v. Seagraves,* 265 F.2d 876, 880 (3d Cir. 1959) (finding theft of geophysical maps identifying possible oil deposits falls under NSPA).

75.   Simon, S. (1998). The Economic Espionage Act of 1996. *Berkeley Technology Law Journal,* 13, 305-306. (explaining history of National Stolen Property Act).

76.   18 U.S.C. §§ 1341, 1343 (2000) (describing elements of mail or wire fraud crimes). For a more extensive discussion of the mail and wire fraud statutes, see the Mail And Wire Fraud Article in this issue.

77.   The mail fraud statute is flexible because almost any use of the mail brings one under the statute's prohibitions. See *Schmuck v. United States,* 489 United States 705, 710-11(1989) (holding use of mails need not be essential part of scheme but only "step in [the] plot").

78.   See *United States v. McNeive,* 536 F.2d 1245, 1247 (1976) (construing statute in light of its manifest purpose to prohibit all attempts to defraud by any form of misrepresentation).

79.   See *United States v. Henry,* 29 F.3d 112, 114 (3d Cir. 1994) ("The statutes cover schemes to defraud another of intangible property, such as confidential business information.").

80. Hsieh, L., McCarthy, J. and Monkus, E. (1998). Intellectual property crimes. *American Criminal Law Review*, 35, 899-920.

81. 18 U.S.C. §§ 1961-1968 (2000) (criminalizing racketeer influenced and corrupt organizations activities). For a full discussion of §§ 1961-1968, see the Racketeer Influenced And Corrupt Organizations article in this issue.

82. E.g., *Religious Tech. Ctr. v. Wollersheim*, 796 F.2d 1076, 1084 (9th Cir. 1986) (recognizing civil RICO claims for trade secret theft but finding injunctive relief not available in RICO action before court). The issue of whether RICO claims give rise to injunctive relief is now before the Supreme Court. See *Scheidler v. Nat'l Org. for Women, Inc.*, 535 United States 1016 (2002).

83. See 18 U.S.C. § 1961(1)(B) (2000) (identifying predicate offenses under RICO which violate criminal law); see also *W. Assocs. Ltd. P'ship v. Mkt. Square Assocs.*, 235 F.3d 629, 633 (1)12, Cir. 2001) (finding predicate offenses are acts punishable under certain state and federal criminal laws).

84. 18 U.S.C. § 1341 (2000).

85. 18 U.S.C. § 1343 (2000).

86. 18 U.S.C. § 2314 (2000).

87. 18 U.S.C. § 2315 (2000). One commentator reports that Congress intended the criminal misappropriation of trade secrets to be a crime punishable under RICO, and thinks it likely that this will occur in the future. See Coblenz, M. (1999). Intellectual property crimes. *Albany Law Journal of Science and Technology*, 9, 235-283 (speculating that Economic Espionage Act (EAA) was not included in RICO amendments because the EEA was signed into law three months after RICO).

88. See *United States v. LaMacchia*, 871 F. Supp. 535, 539 (D. Mass. 1994) (requiring commercial exploitation for criminal offense of software piracy). Saunders, M. J. (1994). Criminal copyright infringement and the Copyright Felony Act. *Denver University Law Review*, 71, 671-672 (discussing requirements for criminal copyright infringement); Spanner, R.A. (1995). The brave new world of criminal software infringement prosecutions. *Computer Law*, 12, 1-11. (discussing various factors involved in criminal software prosecutions); Walker, K. (1994). Federal criminal remedies for the theft of intellectual property. *Hastings Communication & Entertainment Law Journal*, 16, 681-683. (presenting United States Attorney's view on factors for prosecuting high-technology crime as distinguished from civil infringement).

89. See, e.g., *LaMacchia*, 871 F. Supp. at 539-40 (discussing history of criminal copyright law); Saunders, M. J. (1994). Criminal copyright infringement and the Copyright Felony Act. *Denver University Law Review*, 71, 671-680 at 679-80 (describing criminal copyright statute).

90. Pub. L. No. 102-561, 106 Stat. 4233 (codified as amended at 18 U.S.C. §2319(b)-(c) (2000)). For an in-depth discussion of the legislative history of the Copyright Felony Act; Saunders, M. J. (1994). Criminal copyright infringement and the Copyright Felony Act. *Denver University Law Review*, 71, 671-680 at 679-80

91. Hsieh, L., McCarthy, J. and Monkus, E. (1998). Intellectual property crimes. *American Criminal Law Review*, 35, 899-914.

92. Ibid.

93. Hsieh, L., McCarthy, J. and Monkus, E. (1998). Intellectual property crimes. *American Criminal Law Review*, 35, 899-915 at 915.

94. Ibid.

95. See 18 U.S.C. § 1956(c)(7)(D) (2000 & Supp. 2001) (amended to insert section 1030, relating to computer fraud and abuse). For further discussion of this statute

and its applicability to copyright law, see the Money Laundering article in this issue.

96.   The WCO is based in Brussels, Belgium. Established in 1952 as the Customs Cooperation Council, it changed its name in 1994 to World Customs Organization to reflect its worldwide role as the exclusive intergovernmental organization with competence in customs matters. As this is written, there are 151 member governments. WCO hosts a joint Customs/Business IPR Committee, in which business members work directly with governments to enhance enforcement of IPRs and the fight against counterfeiting and piracy.

97.   Interpol was set up to globally enhance and facilitate cross-border criminal police cooperation. It is an international organization with 179 member countries.

98.   See more at www.interpol.int.

99.   McKenzie, S. (1998). Comment, global protection of trademark intellectual property rights: A comparison of infringement and remedies. In China versus the European Union. *Gonzaga Law Review*, 34, 529-539.

100.   McKenzie, S. (1998). Comment, global protection of trademark intellectual property rights: A comparison of infringement and remedies. In China versus the European Union. *Gonzaga Law Review*, 34, 529-539.

101.   Getlan, M. (1995). TRIPS and the future of section 301: A comparative study in trade dispute resolution. *Columbia Journal of Transnational Law*, 34, 173-176.

102.   Countries not in compliance with the set standard would be expected to amend their laws to coincide with international standards and would have to agree to be bound by a dispute settlement mechanism (which would allow retaliatory measures).

103.   Getlan, M. (1995). TRIPS and the future of section 301: A comparative study in trade dispute resolution. *Columbia Journal of Transnational Law*, 34, 173-176.

104.   Rangel-Ortiz, H. (1996). Intellectual property and NAFTA. *Currents: International Trade Law Journal*, 36, 36.

105.   The Uruguay Round was the eighth round sponsored by GATT. General Agreement on Tariffs and Trade -Multilateral Trade Negotiations (The Uruguay Round): Agreement Establishing the Multilateral Trade Organization [World Trade Organization], 15 December 1993, 33 I.L.M. 13.

106.   The World Trade Organization. What is the WTO? Retrieved February 28, 2003 from, http://www.wto. org/english/thewto_e/whatis_e/whatis_e.htm.

107.   (1994). The "author" of the agreement appears to be multiple countries involved with GATT (http://www.wto.org/english/thewto_e/gattmem_e.htm). Agreement on trade-related aspects of intellectual property rights: Agreement on trade-related aspects of intellectual property rights. Retrieved February 3, 2005 from, http://www.wto.org/english/tratop_e/trips_e/ t_agm0_e.htm.

108.   The World Trade Organization. The WTO ...in brief. Retrieved February 3, 2005 from, http://www.wto.org/ english/thewto_e/whatis_e/inbrief_e/inbr00_e.htm.

109.   Hicks, L. & Holbein, J. (1997). Convergence of national intellectual property norms in international trading agreements. *American University Journal of International Law and Policy*, 12, 769-780.

110.   (1994). The "author" of the agreement appears to be multiple countries involved with GATT (http://www.wto.org/english/thewto_e/gattmem_e.htm). Agreement on trade-related aspects of intellectual property rights: Agreement on trade-related aspects of intellectual property rights. Retrieved February 29, 2003 from, http://www.wto.org/english/tratop_e/trips_e/ t_agm0_e.htm.

111.   (1994). The "author" of the agreement appears to be multiple countries involved with GATT (http://www.wto.org/english/thewto_e/gattmem_e.htm). Agreement on trade-related aspects of intellectual property rights: Agreement on trade-related

aspects of intellectual property rights. Retrieved February 29, 2003 from, http://www.wto.org/english/tratop_e/trips_e/ t_agm0_e.htm.

112. Emmert, F. (1990). Intellectual property in the Uruguay Round: Negotiating strategies of the western industrialized countries. *Michigan Journal of International Law*, 11, 1317-79.

113. Emmert, F. (1990). Intellectual property in the Uruguay Round: Negotiating strategies of the western industrialized countries. *Michigan Journal of International Law*, 11, 1317-22. Bello, J. & Holmer, A. (1989-90). "Special 301": Its requirements, implementation, and significance. *Fordham International Law Journal*, 13, 259-260.

114. Oddi, A. (1987). The international patent system and third world development: Reality or myth? *Duke Law Journal*, 831, 848-55. Mossinghoff, G. (1987). Research-based pharmaceutical companies: The need for improved patent protection worldwide. *Journal of Law and Technology*, 2, 307-11.

115. Oddi, A. (1987). The international patent system and third world development: Reality or myth? *Duke Law Journal*, 831, 848-55.

116. Emmert, F. (1990). Intellectual property in the Uruguay Round: Negotiating strategies of the western industrialized countries. *Michigan Journal of International Law*, 11, 1317 at 1354.

117. Hyde, Henry J. Opening Remarks before the Committee on International Relations; *Intellectual property crimes: Are proceeds from counterfeited goods funding terrorism?* (16 July 2003). Retrieved March 25, 2004 from, www.fnsg.com.

118. Interview conducted by author with Wolfgang Starein, Director, World Intellectual Property Organization, Geneva, Switzerland, (2004).

119. Ibid.

120. Ibid.

121. Ibid.

122. Interview conducted by author with Wolfgang Starein, Director, World Intellectual Property Organization, Geneva, Switzerland, (2004).

123. Kastenmeir, W. & Beier, D. (1989). International trade and intellectual property: Promise, risks, and realty. *Vanderbuilt Journal of Transnational Law*, 22, 285-304. The problem with setting time limits to the incentives is that real hardships will ensue if incentives are terminated before real benefits outweigh the costs of the imposed intellectual property system.

124. Some authors have suggested the use of an incentive system, but have emphasized that the incentives must be strictly limited in time so that the developing countries will be encouraged to progress quickly to true intellectual property protection.

125. Niemeyer, K. (1995). Protecting foreign copyright in the People's Republic of China, *Currents: International Trade Law Journal 10, 10.*

126. *Interview conducted by author with Wolfgang Starein, Director, World Intellectual Property Organization, Geneva, Switzerland, (2004).*

127. Ibid.

128. Ibid.

129. Ibid.

130. See Article 11 of the WIPO Copyright Treaty and Article 18 of the WIPO Performances and Phonograms Treaty. Both treaties were adopted by the Diplomatic Conference on Certain Copyright and Neighboring Rights Questions, which was convened under the auspices of WIPO in Geneva on 20 December 1996.

131. Interviews conducted by author with David Mahon, Supervisory Special Agent, Cyber Crime Squad, Federal Bureau of Investigation—Denver Division, 2004.

6

Report of the Task Force on Intellectual Property

U.S. Department of Justice

In response to the growing threat of intellectual property crime, on March 31, 2004, the Attorney General of the United States announced the creation of the Department of Justice's Task Force on Intellectual Property.

The Task Force was entrusted with a timely and important mission: to examine all of the Department of Justice's intellectual property enforcement efforts and to explore methods for the Justice Department to strengthen its protection of the nation's valuable intellectual resources. A team of legal experts, with a diverse range of expertise and experience, was assembled to tackle this undertaking.

The Task Force formed five working groups, or subcommittees, to explore important areas of intellectual property. These working groups, each comprised of relevant Task Force members and expert staff, were designed to ensure that the results would be thorough, comprehensive, and accurate. The working groups analyzed existing resources and proposed meaningful improvements in the following areas: 1) Criminal Enforcement, 2) International Cooperation, 3) Civil and Antitrust Enforcement, 4) Legislation, and 5) Prevention.[1]

The Task Force also consulted other government agencies and gathered information from multiple sources outside the government, including victims of intellectual property theft, creators of intellectual property, community groups, and academia...

What is Intellectual Property?

America builds upon human innovation and creativity. People, inspired by new ideas or artistic visions, create books for us to read, music for us to listen to, and products that improve our lives. Whether they produce movies, design fashion, or develop chemical compounds, these individuals all contribute the creations of their intellect for the nation's benefit.

Just as the law grants ownership rights over material possessions, such as a home or a bicycle, it similarly grants individuals legal rights over intangible property, such as an idea or an invention. When a person creates something that is novel and unique, the law recognizes its value and grants the creator the respect and integrity of ownership for this intellectual property.

Intellectual property permeates everything we do, and its diversity is reflected in the four distinct areas of law that protect it: copyrights, trademarks, trade secrets, and patents.

Copyrights

Written works form the first broad category of protected intellectual property. Books, music, movies, artwork, and plays, for example, are all protected by copyrights, which ensure that the creator of the work can claim authorship and financially benefit from his or her work (for a limited term, usually until seventy years after the author's death). Copyright protection ensures that no one else can claim credit for the work, and the creator is therefore granted the exclusive rights to his or her creation...

Since Congress enacted the first criminal law protecting intellectual property in 1909, federal law enforcement's role has evolved to reflect the changing technologies and media of expression and distribution. The Internet has greatly revolutionized the ability to share information, but at the same time it offers copyright offenders a vast resource for illegally copying and distributing creative works to which they have no rights. In addition, intellectual property enforcement has become a global problem reaching countries all over the world. Consequently, several international agreements exist to coordinate copyright and other intellectual property protections.

Trademarks

In addition to protecting creative works, intellectual property law also protects trademarks. A trademark is any trait used to identify and distinguish products, services, or their producers. McDonald's golden arches and the Nike "swoosh," for example, are commonly recognized trademarks that immediately identify the companies they represent. Trademarks protect the integrity and uniqueness of a product by allowing a consumer to distinguish one product from another. The trademark may be part of the item or its packaging, and may include a distinctive symbol, word, name, sign, shape, or color; even sounds and smells may be part of a trademark. Generic terms, like "soap," however, do not qualify as trademarks.

Manufacturers who have developed a good brand image and a reputation of high quality can rely on their trademark to prevent others from capitalizing on their successes, and to ensure that customers can continue to purchase those same manufacturers' products. Trademarks, therefore, contribute to fair competition in the marketplace. Consumers, on the other hand, rely on trademarks to differentiate between products, and to select those whose reputations they most trust. Trademark protection is therefore the most widely applied intellectual property system both by small businesses and in developing economies...

Trade Secrets

A trade secret is any information used by a business that has some independent economic value that motivates those who possess the information to keep it secret. The recipes for Coca-Cola and Pepsi, for example, are trade secrets that are protected. Trade secrets are far broader in scope than patents, and include scientific or technological information, business information, such as marketing strategies, and even information on "what-not-to-do," such as failed or defective inventions. When the information is obtained through legitimate means, however, it can be freely used. For example, a scientist who reverse-engineers a product and discovers how it is assembled can legally use that information to re-create the product. Furthermore, trade secret protection applies only while secrecy is maintained. Once the secret is publicly disclosed, it loses its legal protection.

Patents

The final major category of intellectual property protection is the patent. From the composition of a new drug to the latest time-saving gadget, patents protect the world of inventions. Laws of nature and natural phenomena, such as gravity and acceleration, however, are not eligible for patent protection, as they are not human creations.

While there are no federal criminal laws that protect patents, there are federal civil laws that protect against patent infringement, and the United States government has numerous international agreements with foreign countries to protect patents.

Misuse of Intellectual Property

Misusing copyrighted material, stealing trade secrets, or counterfeiting trademarked products is a crime. Just as intellectual property has become more and more important for the economy and security of the United States, misuse of intellectual property has become easier and easier, and the consequences are devastating: people are deceived, property is stolen, and businesses are harmed. Consequently, federal laws that criminalize violations of intellectual property rights are fundamentally consistent with other criminal laws, which aim to protect property, deter fraud, and encourage market stability…

Why is Intellectual Property Protection Important?

Ideas and the people who generate them serve as critical resources both in our daily lives and in the stability and growth of America's economy. The creation of intellectual property—from designs for new products to artistic creations—unleashes our nation's potential, brings ideas from concept to commerce, and drives future economic and productivity gains. In the increasingly knowledge-driven, information-age economy, intellectual property is the new coin of the realm, and a key consideration in day-to-day business decisions.

When intellectual property is misappropriated, the consequences are far more devastating than one might imagine. First, intellectual property theft threatens the very foundation of a dynamic, competitive, and stable economy. Second, intellectual property theft can physically endanger our health and safety. As the examples that open this report illustrate, illegal products are often destructive products. Finally, those who benefit most from intellectual property theft are criminals, and alarmingly, criminal organizations with possible ties to terrorism. This is why an effective legal system that defines and protects intellectual property in all its diversity is essential. Intellectual property theft is dangerous and harmful, and we must protect ourselves from the criminals of the new millennium who steal the ideas and hard work of others.

Intellectual property thieves profit—not at the expense of a narrow segment of our society—but at the expense of a wide spectrum of artists, manufacturers, distributors, retailers, company employees, and consumers, as well as the government. The statistics are staggering. According to the Office of the United States Trade Representative, intellectual property theft worldwide costs American companies $250 billion a year. Moreover, as a direct result of counterfeit products and Internet theft of intellectual property, the American economy is losing hundreds of millions of dollars in tax revenues, wages, investment dollars, as well as hundreds of thousands of jobs.

Unfortunately, the harmful consequences of these crimes become even more tangible when we examine cases of counterfeit merchandise. Many people assume that the world of counterfeit and stolen intellectual property is limited to fake "designer" purses, bootleg DVDs for sale on a street corner, or music available for download on the Internet. In reality, counterfeit luxury goods and entertainment products are only a small part of the problem. Intellectual property thieves target highly identifiable, commonly used, and respected trademarked items, such as prescription drugs, automobile and airplane parts, batteries, insecticides, and food products. Criminals falsely duplicate these everyday objects, often substituting cheap filler for a product's real ingredients, to mislead the public into using potentially harmful items...

How has the Department of Justice Attacked the Global Threat of Intellectual Property Crime?

In recent years, the Justice Department has made the enforcement of intellectual property laws a high priority, and in turn has developed a team of specially-trained prosecutors who focus specifically on intellectual property crimes.

The Department of Justice's intellectual property enforcement team includes prosecutors in the Criminal Division's Computer Crime and Intellectual Property Section ("CCIPS"). Based in Washington, DC, this team of specialists serves as a coordinating hub for national and international efforts against intellectual property theft.

Additionally, to combat the widespread nature of intellectual property crime, the Justice Department has assigned specialized prosecutors, called "Computer and Telecommunications Coordinators" ("CTCs"), to all ninety-four United States Attorney's Offices located in geographic subdivisions throughout the nation. These front-line federal prosecutors are directly responsible for handling intellectual property prosecutions in the field.

Finally, the Justice Department has concentrated additional intellectual property theft prosecutors in regions of the country where intellectual property enforcement is especially critical. In these cities, specialized "Computer Hacking and Intellectual Property" ("CHIP") Units have been created to concentrate the number of prosecutors to reflect the intellectual property theft problem in the region.

Computer Crime and Intellectual Property Section ("CCIPS")

With the support of Congress, the Computer Crime and Intellectual Property Section has grown from twenty-two attorneys to more than thirty-five attorneys over the past two years. Created in 1991, CCIPS attorneys prosecute intellectual property cases and provide guidance and training to prosecutors in the field. CCIPS also advises Congress on the development and drafting of intellectual property legislation and provides other policy guidance. Finally, CCIPS prosecutors develop relationships with international law enforcement agencies and foreign prosecutors to strengthen the global response to intellectual property theft.

Computer and Telecommunications Coordinators ("CTCs")

A national network of high-tech federal prosecutors, designated "Computer and Telecommunications Coordinators," exists in all ninety-four United States Attorney's Offices. These federal prosecutors are responsible for prosecuting computer crime and intellectual property cases, training agents and prosecutors, and promoting public awareness programs in their geographic region. Today, there are about 190 CTCs in the field, as many offices have two or more prosecutors dedicated to intellectual property prosecutions. Each prosecutor receives specialized training at an annual conference, and many attend additional seminars at the Department of Justice's National Advocacy Center in Columbia, South Carolina.

Computer Hacking and Intellectual Property Units ("CHIP Units")

Because certain areas of the country have high concentrations of computer crime and intellectual property cases, the Justice Department created "Computer Hacking and Intellectual Property" ("CHIP") Units in those regions. The first of these was launched in February 2000 in the United States Attorney's Office in San Jose,

California, which is responsible for handling cases in the high-tech region of Silicon Valley. In July 2001, the Attorney General expanded the program by creating twelve new CHIP Units in Los Angeles; San Diego; Atlanta; Boston; New York (Brooklyn and Manhattan); Dallas; Seattle; Alexandria, Virginia; Miami; Chicago; and Kansas City, Missouri. In addition to prosecuting computer crime and intellectual property cases, the CHIP teams work closely with local intellectual property industries to prevent computer crime and intellectual property offenses, and also train federal, state, and local prosecutors and investigators. There are currently sixty prosecutors assigned to thirteen existing CHIP Units. In total, the Department of Justice has dedicated more than 250 federal prosecutors around the country to prosecute computer crime and intellectual property theft.

Investigative Resources

Successful criminal prosecutions require reliable investigative resources. Within the Department of Justice, Special Agents of the Federal Bureau of Investigation ("FBI") serve as the primary, and largest, group of investigators working with federal prosecutors. To address the increasing importance of computer crime and intellectual property, in June 2002 the FBI created a new Cyber Division and Intellectual Property Rights Unit that specifically investigates intellectual property theft and fraud. In addition, trained teams of computer forensic experts analyze digital evidence in FBI computer labs and field offices throughout the country. The FBI also has an extensive network of international partnerships with foreign countries and assigns special agents as legal attachés in United States embassies throughout the world.

The Department of Justice also works closely with numerous local and state police officers and other federal law enforcement agencies, including the United States Secret Service, the Bureau of Immigration and Customs Enforcement, and the United States Postal Inspection Service.

The Secret Service seeks to protect America's financial and telecommunications infrastructure, which is increasingly exploited by intellectual property criminals. The Secret Service's Criminal Investigative Division has an Electronic Crimes Section that supports thirteen Electronic Crimes Task Forces in select cities where local, state, and federal law enforcement officers investigate numerous types of high-tech crimes.

The Bureau of Immigration and Customs Enforcement is an investigative arm of the Department of Homeland Security, and assists federal prosecutors with the seizure of counterfeit goods at the nation's borders and ports-of-entry.

Finally, as the primary law enforcement arm of the United States Postal Service, the Postal Inspection Service performs postal investigative and security functions, which become especially important in the investigation of trafficking in counterfeit goods.

Intellectual Property Prosecutions

Working together, the specially-trained federal prosecutors of the Department of Justice and the dedicated agents of federal, state, and local law enforcement agencies have formed a formidable team against intellectual property criminals. Over the past several years, the Department of Justice and its law enforcement partners have prosecuted numerous intellectual property thieves and dismantled criminal networks that presented a serious threat to the nation's economic security and the personal well-being of Americans. Some of these cases include the following:

- Counterfeit Baby Formula: In August 2002, a California man was sentenced to over three years in prison for selling thousands of cases of counterfeit infant formula to wholesale grocers.
- Counterfeit Pharmaceuticals: In January 2004, two California men were prosecuted for manufacturing 700,000 fake Viagra tablets valued at $5.6 million, and for attempting to sell the fake drugs in the United States. One defendant has pleaded guilty and is awaiting sentencing, while the other defendant is awaiting trial for his alleged role in the scheme.
- Counterfeit Pesticides: In January 2004, an Alabama man was sentenced to over three years in prison and ordered to pay $45,000 in restitution for selling mislabeled and adulterated pesticides to city governments and private businesses, which used the pesticides to try to control mosquitos harboring the deadly West Nile virus in a number of southern and mid-western states.
- Counterfeit Designer Clothing: In 2003, a South Carolina man was sentenced to seven years in prison and ordered to pay $3.5 million in restitution for selling fake Nike shoes and Tommy Hilfiger apparel.
- Counterfeit Software: In December 2003, a Virginia man was sentenced to over five years in prison and ordered to pay $1.7 million in restitution for distributing more than $7 million in counterfeit software over the Internet. In a separate prosecution in April 2004, a Ukranian man was charged with illegally distributing millions of dollars of unauthorized copies of software from Microsoft, Adobe,

Autodesk, Borland, and Macromedia. The government of Thailand recently extradited the defendant to the United States to face criminal charges.

- Bootleg Recordings: In July 2004, a Pittsburgh man was sentenced to over a year in prison and fined $120,000 for illegally copying and selling 11,000 video and audio recordings of live musical acts by such artists as KISS, Aerosmith, Bob Dylan, and Bruce Springsteen...

What Can the Department of Justice do to Expand the Fight against Intellectual Property Crime?

A. Criminal Enforcement Recommendations

The United States Department of Justice makes enforcement of the criminal intellectual property laws a high priority. The Justice Department prosecutes criminal cases involving the theft of copyrighted works, trademark counterfeiting, and theft of trade secrets. Many divisions and offices of the Justice Department participate in the enforcement of intellectual property laws, including federal prosecutors located throughout the nation. These prosecutors work closely with local, state, and federal law enforcement agents to identify criminals and prosecute them in accordance with the law.

While the Department of Justice has successfully prosecuted numerous intellectual property cases over the past several years, the Task Force believes additional success is possible...

Criminal Enforcement Recommendation #1

Expand the CHIP Program by Adding Five New Units

Recommendation: *The Department of Justice should create five additional CHIP Units in regions of the country where intellectual property producers significantly contribute to the national economy. These areas are 1) the District of Columbia; 2) Sacramento, California; 3) Pittsburgh, Pennsylvania; 4) Nashville, Tennessee; and 5) Orlando, Florida.*

Background: In July 2001, the Attorney General created the Computer Hacking and Intellectual Property ("CHIP") Program based on the success of the model CHIP Unit existing in the United States Attorney's Office in San Jose, California. The CHIP Program requires prosecutors to focus on copyright and trademark violations, theft of trade secrets, computer intrusions, theft of computer and high-tech components, and Internet fraud. In addition, CHIP Unit prosecutors are expected to develop public awareness programs and provide training to other prosecutors and law enforcement agencies regarding high-tech issues.

The Attorney General expanded the CHIP Program by creating ten additional units in strategic regions of the country where, similar to San Jose, California, intellectual property offenses and computer crime were most prevalent. Using funds provided by Congress for the 2001 fiscal year, the Justice Department added twenty-eight positions for prosecutors and assigned them to ten offices to create new CHIP Units. In addition to the new positions, each office assigned existing prosecutors to the CHIP Unit. In total, the 10 CHIP Units created in 2001 consisted of forty-eight CHIP Unit positions for prosecutors. In 2002, the Attorney General expanded the program once more and created CHIP Units in Chicago, Miami, and Kansas City, Missouri. As a result, the CHIP Program currently consists of Units in thirteen offices with approximately sixty prosecutors dedicated to computer crime and intellectual property enforcement.

Explanation: The Task Force has found that the CHIP program has been very successful in increasing the effectiveness of the Justice Department's intellectual property enforcement efforts. During the 2003 fiscal year, the first full year after all thirteen of the CHIP Units became operational, the offices with CHIP Units filed charges against 46 percent more defendants than they had averaged in the four fiscal years prior to the formation of the units.

This increase in intellectual property prosecutions in districts with CHIP Units can be linked to several factors. First, many districts have large populations and strong business sectors that are frequently victimized by intellectual property crime. In addition, the creation of a specialized unit in the area visibly conveys the Department of Justice's commitment to prosecuting intellectual property crime. As a result, more victims have reported intellectual property crimes and cooperated with law enforcement authorities. Moreover, CHIP Units have developed local policies, guidelines, and strategies to address specific intellectual property crime issues in their regions. Consequently, the strategically tailored and focused approach to a particular region in areas with CHIP Units is more likely to result in a higher number of enforcement actions.

The Department of Justice should expand the CHIP Program by adding units in areas of the country where intellectual property resources significantly contribute to the national economy. These areas should have intellectual property concerns that can be addressed with intellectual property enforcement efforts, such as a large population of potential victims and a history of intellectual property offenses in the area. Accordingly, the Task Force recommends the creation of new units in the following five areas: 1) the District of Columbia, home to numerous sensitive government computer systems that contain the nation's intellectual property; 2) Sacramento, California (population 6.8 million), which has significant high-tech sectors; 3) Pittsburgh, Pennsylvania (population almost 4 million), which also has significant high-tech sectors; 4) Nashville, Tennessee, home to one of the largest recording industries in the world, including the country music industry; and 5) Orlando, Florida (population 8.9 million), an expanding region with a history of intellectual property prosecutions.

Each of these areas has business sectors that generate significant intellectual property resources and are often victimized by intellectual property crime. The creation of CHIP Units in these areas should significantly increase the Justice Department's intellectual property efforts.

Criminal Enforcement Recommendation #2

Reinforce and Expand CHIP Units in Key Regions

Recommendation: *The Department of Justice should reinforce and expand existing CHIP Units located in key regions where intellectual property offenses have increased, and where the CHIP Units have effectively developed programs to prosecute CHIP-related cases, coordinate law enforcement activity, and promote public awareness programs.*

Background: Two regions of the country have had particularly significant intellectual property problems. The Central District of California, consisting of the Los Angeles metropolitan area, is the largest district in the United States and has a population of approximately 18 million. The district includes the largest sea port in the world, is home to the entertainment industry, and includes numerous high-tech businesses and universities. The existing CHIP Unit in Los Angeles has prosecuted 10 percent of all intellectual property cases in the United States from 1998 through 2003 and 24 percent of the cases prosecuted by the thirteen offices with CHIP Units during the same period.

The Northern District of California, which contains San Jose and San Francisco, ranks second in the number of intellectual property cases prosecuted in the country. The district has approximately 7.5 million people and includes numerous high-tech companies that produce a large amount of intellectual property resources. The existing CHIP unit has also handled several important theft of trade secret cases and recently achieved the unprecedented extradition of a defendant in an international software theft case.

Both the San Jose and Los Angeles regions have a large economic base and numerous actual and potential victims of intellectual property theft. Both offices have extensive public awareness programs, and the economies of both districts are highly dependent on the protection and enforcement of intellectual property rights. Accordingly, the Department of Justice should expand and reinforce the CHIP Units in these two districts with new prosecutors who can respond to the significant intellectual property enforcement needs in these regions.

Criminal Enforcement Recommendation #3

Designate CHIP Coordinators in Every Federal Prosecutor's Office in the Nation

Recommendation: *The Department of Justice should designate CHIP Coordinators in every federal prosecutor's office and make the coordinators responsible for intellectual property enforcement in that region.*

Background: In 1995, the Department of Justice created the Computer and Telecommunications Coordinator ("CTC") Program, which designated at least one federal prosecutor to prosecute cyber crime and intellectual property theft within each district. In addition, CTCs were made responsible for providing technical advice to fellow prosecutors, assisting other CTCs in multi-district investigations, and coordinating public awareness efforts.

CTCs receive special training and participate in an annual CTC conference. During the CTC conference, participants receive training in both computer and intellectual property-related areas and meet with other CTCs to coordinate investigations and exchange ideas. When the Attorney General created the CHIP Units, those thirteen offices replaced the CTC positions with CHIP prosecutors. The remaining United States Attorney's Offices without CHIP Units continued to designate prosecutors as CTCs.

Explanation: The re-designation from CTC to CHIP Coordinator will align all ninety-four U.S. Attorney's Offices with the Attorney General's CHIP program announced in 2001, and the enforcement mission of the Computer Crime and Intellectual Property Section in Washington, DC. The addition of "Intellectual Property" in the title will further clarify the coordinator's responsibility to prosecute intellectual property offenses and coordinate public awareness and training efforts within the district. A CHIP Coordinator in every office will also provide a designated contact for law enforcement agents and victims of intellectual property crime. Consequently, the Department of Justice should be able to increase intellectual property prosecutions and effectively coordinate enforcement efforts.

Criminal Enforcement Recommendation #4

Examine the Need to Increase CCIPS Resources

Recommendation: *The Department of Justice should examine the need to increase resources for the Computer Crime and Intellectual Property Section of the Criminal Division in Washington, DC, to address additional intellectual property enforcement concerns.*

Background: The past three years have seen a marked evolution in the development of the Criminal Division's intellectual property rights enforcement efforts. Specifically, the Computer Crime and Intellectual Property Section ("CCIPS") has made the development, investigation, and prosecution of large-scale, multi-national intellectual property cases a singular priority. As a result, CCIPS has pursued several significant intellectual property law enforcement actions. In addition, CCIPS has developed comprehensive programs and policies to address important aspects of intellectual property enforcement, including domestic and international issues, and provided advice to lawmakers.

Explanation: Currently there are twelve prosecutors in CCIPS dedicated to the enforcement of intellectual property rights. Particularly in light of the increasing necessity to focus the Justice Department's efforts on large-scale, multi-national, and multi-district prosecutions, such as Operations Buccaneer and Fastlink, it is critical to ensure that CCIPS has sufficient resources to prosecute, coordinate, and otherwise provide assistance and expertise to high-priority intellectual property cases. In addition, because of the Department of Justice's increased efforts to enhance international cooperation, additional resources are particularly necessary. Accordingly, the Justice Department should examine the need for additional prosecutors for CCIPS.

Criminal Enforcement Recommendation #5

Increase the Number of FBI Agents Assigned to Intellectual Property Investigations

Recommendation: *The Department of Justice should recommend that the FBI increase the number of Special Agents assigned to intellectual property investigations, as the Justice Department itself increases the number of prosecutors assigned to intellectual property enforcement.*

Background: The Task Force has recommended that the Department of Justice expand the number of CHIP Units and prosecutors who handle intellectual property prosecutions. Additional prosecutions, however, are dependent upon the number of investigative agents assigned to respond to intellectual property crimes.

The FBI has proven its tremendous investigative and technical capabilities in numerous, complex intellectual property cases prosecuted by the Department of Justice, including multi-district investigations and sophisticated enforcement actions. In addition, FBI agents are on the front line of criminal investigations, and they are typically the first responders when trade secret thefts or other intellectual property crimes are reported.

Explanation: The FBI should continue to develop intellectual property cases and increase the number of agents who are dedicated to intellectual property investigations. As the volume of intellectual property crime continues to expand, both the number of prosecutors and the number of investigators must increase. In addition, the FBI should align its investigative resources in the regions where the Justice Department has assigned additional prosecutors to fight intellectual property crime.

Criminal Enforcement Recommendation #6

Increase FBI Personnel Assigned to Search for Digital Evidence

Recommendation: *The Department of Justice should recommend that the FBI increase the number of personnel assigned to search for digital evidence in intellectual property cases.*

Background: Because digital evidence is often the cornerstone of a successful intellectual property prosecution, the government's ability to locate and interpret this evidence is critical. Information found on computers and other digital devices, such as cell phones and personal digital assistants, can often lead to important evidence in an intellectual property case. For example, organized online groups, known as "warez" groups, distribute stolen software, movies, and other copyrighted works using sophisticated computer networks that contain large storage devices. A timely computer forensic examination is often necessary to identify the offenders, analyze the stolen materials, and determine whether additional evidence is needed before criminal charges can be filed.

Explanation: In response to the evolving technological sophistication of intellectual property theft, the FBI should increase its forensic capabilities to maintain its advantage over high-tech intellectual property criminals, who are increasingly using complex computer systems and massive data storage devices. Consequently, digital evidence examination is becoming especially important in the investigative phase of intellectual property cases and the FBI should increase the number of trained personnel capable of addressing this important issue.

Criminal Enforcement Recommendation #7

Target Large, Complex Criminal Organizations That Commit Intellectual Property Crimes

Recommendation: *The Department of Justice should dismantle and prosecute more nationwide and international criminal organizations that commit intellectual property crimes.*

Background: The Department of Justice divides the United States into geographic districts where federal prosecutors are assigned to prosecute crimes within that particular district. Intellectual property theft, however, is a crime that is not limited by the borders of a district, state, or nation. Intellectual property is routinely stolen from the United States, sent overseas, manufactured in clandestine factories, and shipped around the world. Internet-related intellectual property theft is even more global because intellectual property thieves can use computer networks to steal, store, and distribute stolen software, motion pictures, music, and other copyrighted material. In addition, the Internet and computer technologies have enabled intellectual property thieves to communicate instantly over thousands of miles through e-mail, chat rooms, instant messaging, and a variety of other methods.

The Task Force recognizes that the Department of Justice has been responsive to the threat of intellectual property. For example, as one part of this important effort, the Department of Justice has developed complex, multi-district, and international enforcement efforts designed to attack this problem. Several of these enforcement efforts have included numerous arrests, searches, and seizures of evidence within a short time period. These coordinated efforts send a strong signal that sophisticated, multiple-defendant criminal organizations are not immune from prosecution. Coordinated operations, such as Operations Buccaneer, Fastlink, Digital Gridlock, and Digital Marauder, involved charges against numerous defendants and required execution of simultaneous searches in dozens of foreign countries. Each of these challenging operations required coordination with several offices within the Department of Justice, law enforcement agencies, and international governments, and in effect, served as a visible deterrent against intellectual property crimes.

Explanation: The Department of Justice should increase the number of complex, multi-district intellectual property enforcement actions to target sophisticated intellectual property thieves and organizations. Because global enforcement is the key to global deterrence, the Department of Justice should continue to work with foreign nations to build on the success of operations involving simultaneous arrests and searches and make them an integral part of future coordinated efforts. These types of challenging, yet important, initiatives should serve as a model for future law enforcement efforts to attack intellectual property crime.

Criminal Enforcement Recommendation #8

Enhance Training Programs for Prosecutors and Law Enforcement Agents

Recommendation: *The Department of Justice should enhance programs to train prosecutors and law enforcement agents investigating intellectual property offenses.*

Background: The nature of intellectual property crime is constantly changing. Counterfeiters quickly change their methods to conceal their illicit activity. Copyright infringers rapidly adapt to security measures placed on music, DVDs, or software that are intended to deter illegal copying. Criminal networks swiftly modify communication techniques, distribution channels, and other methods of advancing their criminal activity.

Law enforcement must constantly adapt to these changing criminal methods. To address this concern, the Department of Justice conducts training on a wide variety of legal and technical intellectual property issues. For example, each year the Justice Department sponsors a conference for all prosecutors involved in intellectual property and computer crime enforcement. During this conference, prosecutors from across the country learn about changes in the law and exchange ideas about enforcement efforts. In addition, the Department of Justice sponsors a course at its National Advocacy Center in Columbia, South Carolina, to educate prosecutors and emphasize that intellectual property enforcement is a federal priority.

Department of Justice prosecutors also provide intellectual property training for local, state, and federal law enforcement agents.

This training involves presentations on intellectual property law, investigative approaches, and the changing methods of intellectual property criminals. The FBI also sponsors an annual course at its training academy in Quantico, Virginia, for special agents assigned to investigate intellectual property offenses.

Explanation: Because training and preparation are keys to an effective and swift enforcement plan, the Department of Justice should enhance training opportunities and programs for prosecutors and investigators assigned to intellectual property enforcement. With rapidly changing technology and criminal methods, it is essential that the Justice Department constantly review its training courses, and offer additional training courses to advance the government's ongoing emphasis on intellectual property enforcement.

Criminal Enforcement Recommendation #9

Prosecute Intellectual Property Offenses That Endanger the Public's Health or Safety

Recommendation: *The Department of Justice should prosecute aggressively intellectual property offenses that endanger the public's health or safety.*

Background: It is clear that intellectual property crime can pose a serious health and safety risk to the public, from batteries with dangerously high levels of mercury that can find their way into children's toys, to fake medicines and pesticides that can harm unsuspecting consumers. Accordingly, the criminals who counterfeit these items and place the public at risk must be prosecuted aggressively and to the fullest extent of the law. Federal laws have been enacted to give prosecutors necessary legal tools to hold criminals accountable for such conduct. As the sheer volume of fake goods that are harmful to public health and safety continues to rise, it is important to dedicate the level of resources necessary to deter the intellectual property criminals threatening our public health and safety.

Explanation: The Department of Justice should, through a formalized memorandum to prosecutors throughout the country, emphasize the urgency of aggressively prosecuting intellectual property offenses that endanger the health and safety of the public. The Justice Department should continue to commit itself to ensuring the public good, as well as reinforcing consumer confidence in the products that positively affect the welfare of the country. In addition, the Department of Justice should continue to work closely with federal and local agencies, which encounter these products at the nation's borders and in the marketplace, to prosecute those who seek to endanger the public through intellectual property offenses.

Criminal Enforcement Recommendation #10

Emphasize Charging of Intellectual Property Offenses

Recommendation: *The Department of Justice should emphasize the importance of charging intellectual property offenses in every type of investigation where such charges are applicable, including organized crime, fraud, and illegal international smuggling.*

Background: Many crimes involve intellectual property offenses. When the focus of the investigation centers on another serious offense, however, the intellectual property offenses are often not emphasized. For example, a counterfeit drug investigation may result in charges under the federal statutes that prohibit the sale of adulterated pharmaceuticals. In addition, defendants who commit organized crime or fraud offenses where counterfeiting is involved are usually charged with racketeering or fraud violations, sometimes without additional intellectual property charges.

Explanation: Consistent with the Department of Justice's policy that prosecutors must charge the most serious, readily provable offenses, the Task Force believes that the Department of Justice should emphasize that intellectual property offenses should always be charged when appropriate. If an intellectual property offense occurs during the course of other types of criminal activity, such as fraud, organized crime, or international smuggling, prosecutors should also charge the intellectual property offense. The Department of Justice should seek to convict defendants involved in intellectual property offenses regardless of whether the focus of the investigation is on another serious offense, in order to send a message that intellectual property offenses will not be tolerated.

Criminal Enforcement Recommendation #11

Enhance Victim Education Programs and Increase Cooperation

Recommendation: *The Department of Justice should enhance its program of educating and encouraging victims of intellectual property offenses and industry representatives to cooperate in criminal investigations. Recommended enhancements include:*

1) Encouraging victims to report intellectual property crime to law enforcement agencies;
2) Distributing the new "Department of Justice Guide to Reporting Intellectual Property Crime" to victims and industry representatives regarding federal intellectual property offenses; and
3) Hosting a conference with victims and industry representatives to educate participants on how they can assist in law enforcement investigations.

Background: Prosecutors in the Department of Justice have made extensive inroads through public awareness programs to educate victims, consumers, and the law enforcement community that intellectual property enforcement is a priority of the Department of Justice. The Task Force recognizes that combating intellectual property crime requires cooperation among law enforcement, prosecutors, and victims of intellectual property theft, including those who have unwittingly purchased counterfeit or stolen goods.

Explanation: The Department of Justice should enhance its programs to encourage victims of intellectual property offenses and industry representatives to cooperate in criminal investigations. This can be accomplished in three ways. First, Department of Justice prosecutors should continue to develop regional public awareness programs that encourage intellectual property victims to report offenses to federal authorities at the earliest stage possible.

Effective prosecution of intellectual property crime requires substantial assistance from its victims. Because the holders of intellectual property rights are often in the best position to detect a theft, law enforcement authorities cannot act in many cases unless the crimes are promptly reported to them. Once these crimes are reported, federal law enforcement authorities need to identify quickly the facts that establish jurisdiction for the potential offenses, such as federal copyright and trademark registration information, the extent of the victim's potential loss, the nature of the theft, and the identity of possible suspects. In a digital world where evidence can disappear at the click of a mouse, swift investigation is often essential to a successful prosecution.

Second, the Justice Department should extensively distribute the new "Department of Justice Guide to Reporting Intellectual Property Crime." This guide will further educate individuals and industry representatives on how to report intellectual property crime. The accompanying checklist should streamline the process, and assist prosecutors and law enforcement agents in the rapid response to reports of intellectual property crimes.

Finally, the Department of Justice should sponsor a conference to explore how victims and industry representatives can assist law enforcement in fighting intellectual property crime. Victim assistance is a critical factor in the success or failure of an intellectual property investigation. Intellectual property enforcement, however, is a complex and sometimes technically challenging area. The conference should be designed to educate participants, and to exchange ideas on the best methods for attacking the problem of intellectual property theft.

Criminal Enforcement Recommendation #12

Issue Internal Guidance to Federal Prosecutors Regarding How Victims Can Assist Prosecutors in Intellectual Property Cases

Recommendation: *The Department of Justice should issue internal guidance to federal prosecutors regarding how victims can assist prosecutors in intellectual property cases.*

Background: Prosecutions of intellectual property crime often depend on cooperation between victims and law enforcement. Without information-sharing from victims, prosecutors cannot enforce the intellectual property laws. Many industry groups and victims of intellectual property theft are eager to assist law enforcement in finding intellectual property offenders and to bring them to justice. Certain types of assistance, however, such as the donation of funds, property, or services by outside sources to federal law enforcement authorities, can raise potential legal and ethical issues. In general, federal rules and regulations place limitations on the types of assistance victims and outside sources can provide to law enforcement authorities.

Explanation: The Department of Justice should issue internal guidance to Department of Justice prosecutors regarding permissible assistance of victims in intellectual property prosecutions. Victim assistance is a critical factor in the success of an investigation and prosecution of an intellectual property crime. Nevertheless, the Department of Justice must continue its ongoing efforts to educate federal prosecutors about potential legal and ethical issues, in an effort to maintain the Department of Justice's independence and unassailable integrity.

B. International Cooperation Recommendations

The Task Force believes that international cooperation is a critical component in stemming the tide of global intellectual property theft. Intellectual property thieves in foreign countries must be subject to prosecution by foreign governments. In addition, foreign governments must assist the United States in its efforts to gather evidence and prosecute intellectual property criminals who violate the laws of the United States. Accordingly, the Task Force recommends that the Department of Justice adopt the following recommendations to increase cooperation with foreign countries regarding intellectual property enforcement:

International Cooperation Recommendation #1

Deploy Intellectual Property Law Enforcement Coordinators to Asia and Eastern Europe

Recommendation: *The Department of Justice should deploy federal prosecutors to the United States embassies in Hong Kong and Budapest, Hungary, and designate them as "Intellectual Property Law Enforcement Coordinators" ("IPLECs") to coordinate intellectual property enforcement efforts in those regions.*

Background: International cooperation is a major component of a comprehensive intellectual property enforcement program. Many intellectual property offenders operate in countries where the laws are not effective or the relevant expertise of law enforcement is inadequate. Asia and Eastern Europe are areas of particular importance to the creators of intellectual property because of the increasing amount of counterfeiting in the regions.

While developing nations in Asia have increased their manufacturing capacity for legitimate goods, the region has also become a major manufacturer of counterfeit products. Factories in China, Taiwan, and Hong Kong produce numerous counterfeit designer goods and other products protected by United States trademarks. Factories in Singapore and Thailand produce large amounts of counterfeit software and movies that are exported to the United States, sometimes before the films are released to the general public. Consequently, many intellectual property offenses in the United States are traced to manufacturing plants and bank accounts in Asia. In fact, the United States Trade Representative has identified several Southeast Asian countries, such as China, Malaysia, Thailand, Taiwan, Indonesia, and the Philippines, as countries that do not adequately or effectively protect intellectual property rights.

Fortunately, many of these nations are trying to improve the situation and are increasingly cooperative with the United States in its international law enforcement efforts. For example, China has hosted international training programs on intellectual property enforcement and invited Department of Justice officials to participate. In another example, Thailand has extradited to the United States a fugitive accused of intellectual property crimes, and through a joint United States-Hungarian task force on organized crime, Hungary has also cooperated with the Department of Justice and the FBI in attacking international intellectual property offenses.

Explanation: The Department of Justice should encourage the continued cooperation of the governments in Asia and Eastern Europe by assigning a federal prosecutor to the United States embassies in Hong Kong and Budapest, Hungary. The federal prosecutor should have the specific task of coordinating investigations and prosecutions of intellectual property criminals located in the region. The prosecutor should be designated as an "Intellectual Property Law Enforcement Coordinator," or "IPLEC," and should develop relationships with the foreign law enforcement agencies in the region. The IPLEC should also provide legal and technical assistance and develop training programs on intellectual property enforcement. In addition, the IPLEC should assist prosecutors based in the United States by providing direct contact with foreign law enforcement agencies, and assist in intellectual property investigations.

The Department of Justice should recruit federal prosecutors who are experienced in prosecuting intellectual property crimes for placement as the IPLECs in Hong Kong and Budapest, Hungary. In addition, the IPLECs should be a valuable resource in examining intellectual property crime trends in the region.

International Cooperation Recommendation #2

Co-Locate FBI Intellectual Property Legal Attachés to Asia and Eastern Europe

Recommendation: *The Department of Justice should recommend that the FBI colocate Legal Attachés with intellectual property expertise to Hong Kong and Budapest, Hungary, to assist the newly assigned IPLECs in investigative efforts.*

Background: The Federal Bureau of Investigation currently assigns special agents to United States embassies throughout the world. The agents, known as "Legal Attachés," communicate regularly with foreign law enforcement agencies, assist in joint investigations, and provide expertise when requested by the foreign government. Legal Attachés are responsible for assisting in all types of international investigations, from terrorism to computer crime.

Intellectual property investigations are often complex and involve unique technical issues. For example, investigations that target online intellectual property theft often require specialized computer expertise to track down the offenders and locate important evidence. In addition, the schemes and methods used by intellectual property smugglers are often sophisticated and involve complex financial transactions. Consequently, specially-trained investigators are needed to pursue intellectual property offenders who operate in foreign countries.

Explanation: The Department of Justice should recommend that the FBI assign an Intellectual Property Legal Attaché in Hong Kong and Budapest, Hungary, to assist the federal prosecutor assigned as the Intellectual Property Law Enforcement Coordinator for the region. An effective enforcement program requires close coordination between prosecutors and the skilled investigators who gather evidence, interview witnesses, and develop investigative strategies.

An FBI agent assigned as an Intellectual Property Legal Attaché will significantly increase the effectiveness of international enforcement efforts by providing an experienced United States investigator to support international assistance requests, develop relationships with foreign law enforcement agents, and provide investigative expertise to foreign nations. The Intellectual Property Legal Attaché should receive special training in intellectual property investigations and should work closely with the IPLEC to create international partnerships and task forces in the region.

International Cooperation Recommendation #3

Increase the Use of Informal Contacts to Gather Evidence from Foreign Countries

Recommendation: *Direct prosecutors and agents to increase the use of alternative channels of communication, such as "law enforcement-to-law enforcement" contacts to collect information and evidence quickly in foreign investigations.*

Background: International enforcement requires international cooperation in identifying criminal suspects, gathering information from victims, and collecting other types of evidence. The United States has negotiated numerous "Mutual Legal Assistance Treaties" with foreign governments to provide a method to share information and to assist other nations in international criminal investigations. These treaties usually include procedures to interview witnesses and perform other investigative functions. Evidence obtained through formal legal assistance is processed by government agencies in both countries and is typically admissible in United States District Courts. Often, however, investigators need to gather information quickly to determine whether a crime has been committed or to identify criminal suspects before they flee. At that stage of the investigation, it is often unclear whether the case will be prosecuted in the United States or referred to the foreign country where the American rules of evidence do not apply. In addition, evidence that may exist on computers, whether on personal computers or the large networks of foreign Internet Service Providers, is not always preserved and could disappear if immediate action is not taken.

Explanation: While legal assistance treaties provide a reliable mechanism for contacting foreign nations, making information requests, and gathering evidence that is admissible in United States courts, the Department of Justice should explore the use of alternative measures when formal requests are unnecessary, or when the need to gather evidence is time-sensitive. In these situations, law enforcement-to-law enforcement contact should be used to gather information quickly. For example, FBI Legal Attachés assigned to United States embassies often have close working relationships with foreign law enforcement representatives, including national and local police officers. Many times, these "police-to-police" contacts are a much more efficient method to obtain information in criminal investigations, especially when timing is critical. In addition, the police-to-police contacts may open up opportunities for the FBI Legal Attachés to develop relationships with foreign Internet Service Providers, industry representatives, and other commercial contacts where the foreign nation allows such contacts. In many international investigations, Department of Justice prosecutors have also used "prosecutor-to-prosecutor" and "prosecutor-to-police" contacts with their foreign counterparts to gather information and coordinate international enforcement efforts. The Department of Justice should continue to use these important methods of communication with foreign law enforcement, especially in cases where a legal assistance treaty does not exist between the United States and the foreign government. Consequently, a police-to-police, prosecutor-to-prosecutor, or prosecutor-to-police contact can sometimes be the only method to gather evidence quickly in a criminal investigation.

International Cooperation Recommendation #4

Enhance Intellectual Property Training Programs for Foreign Prosecutors and Law Enforcement

Recommendation: *The Department of Justice should enhance its intellectual property training programs for foreign prosecutors and law enforcement investigators in coordination with the Department of State.*

Background: Intellectual property crime is a global problem, but many countries lack the necessary laws, resources, or expertise to enforce intellectual property rights. Numerous foreign countries have yet to develop a legal system to handle intellectual property cases, and many countries that have such laws lack the experience or expertise to prosecute sophisticated offenders. Consequently, foreign prosecutors and investigators are often unable to enforce copyright laws or prosecute large-scale counterfeiters who have stolen the intellectual property of Americans.

Explanation: For the purposes of providing the requisite expertise and enabling the development of critical law enforcement-to-law enforcement relationships, it is essential that the Department of Justice provide additional training and assistance programs to foreign nations focused on intellectual property crimes.

The Department of Justice should identify countries where: 1) intellectual property enforcement would have a significant impact, 2) the foreign governments are willing to create new laws, or modify old ones, to fight intellectual property crimes, and 3) the foreign governments are willing to dedicate resources to fighting intellectual property crime, but lack the expertise to do so.

The Department of Justice should invite these countries to participate in a training program, or series of training programs, to learn about enforcement strategies, receive assistance on drafting new laws, and receive valuable guidance on methods to track down intellectual property criminals. The Justice Department should then further develop the relationships with the participating foreign governments by sending federal prosecutors and investigators to the foreign countries to further assist in the countries' intellectual property enforcement efforts.

International Cooperation Recommendation #5

Prioritize Negotiations for Legal Assistance Treaties

Recommendation: *The Department of Justice should prioritize treaty negotiations for legal assistance agreements with foreign governments where intellectual property enforcement is a significant problem.*

Background: Working in close coordination with the Department of State, the Justice Department is actively involved in negotiating treaties with foreign countries to increase cooperation in criminal investigations. For example, the United States negotiates "Mutual Legal Assistance Treaties" with many nations to create a formal method for exchanging evidence and information. These formal international agreements are useful to prosecutors and law enforcement agents because they provide a method for the Department of Justice to request a foreign government to gather evidence, interview witnesses, and to provide other forms of legal assistance. In addition, a legal assistance treaty imposes an important obligation on the foreign country to assist in criminal investigations in accordance with the international agreement.

Explanation: The Department of Justice should prioritize the negotiation of legal assistance treaties with foreign governments where intellectual property enforcement is a significant problem. For example, the Department of Justice should ensure that it has effective legal assistance treaties with the nations in Asia, where counterfeiting has become a significant problem. Many intellectual property investigations in the United States lead to evidence located in Asian and South Asian countries where American law enforcement agents do not have jurisdiction. Therefore, it is vital that the Department of Justice and other government agencies negotiate legal assistance treaties with these countries to increase international cooperation.

International Cooperation Recommendation #6

Prioritize Negotiations and Include Intellectual Property Crimes in Extradition Treaties

Recommendation: *The Department of Justice should ensure that intellectual property crimes are included in all extradition treaties and prioritize negotiations with foreign countries according to intellectual property enforcement concerns.*

Background: In addition to legal assistance treaties, the Department of Justice is actively involved in negotiating extradition treaties with foreign countries. Extradition treaties provide a formal process for the Department of Justice to bring an alleged criminal to the United States to face criminal charges. The United States currently has extradition treaties with more than 100 countries, and some of these treaties have been in place for decades. In some of the older extradition treaties, the United States is allowed to seek the extradition of an alleged criminal only if the crime charged is one of the crimes listed in the treaty. In newer treaties, however, the United States may generally seek extradition when the crime charged is an offense in both countries. For example, if trafficking in counterfeit goods is a crime in both the United States and the foreign country, an alleged criminal in the foreign country could be extradited to the United States to face those charges.

Explanation: The Department of Justice should work to ensure that intellectual property crimes are included in extradition treaties with foreign countries. The United States should seek to negotiate new extradition treaties with countries where intellectual property enforcement is critical and should seek to re-negotiate treaties when intellectual property offenses are not included in existing agreements. The ability of governments to apprehend intellectual property criminals in foreign nations is a critical factor in whether intellectual property laws can be enforced. Consequently, it is important to have effective international extradition treaties that include intellectual property offenses in order to promote global cooperative efforts.

International Cooperation Recommendation #7

Emphasize Intellectual Property Enforcement during Discussions with Foreign Governments

Recommendation: *The Department of Justice should emphasize intellectual property enforcement issues during discussions with foreign governments.*

Background: The Attorney General and other Department of Justice officials routinely meet and correspond with foreign law enforcement officials to discuss international cooperation on a wide variety of criminal justice issues. For example, the Attorney General frequently meets and corresponds with Justice Ministers in Asia, Europe, and South America.

Explanation: The Department of Justice should, with increased emphasis, raise the issue of intellectual property enforcement with foreign officials, especially in such regions as Asia and Eastern Europe, where enforcement is of concern to the United States. As set forth in other recommendations in this report, the Department of Justice should offer its expertise and assistance in developing robust intellectual property enforcement programs in foreign nations, developing effective legal assistance treaties, and continuing an open dialogue about emerging intellectual property issues.

C. Civil Enforcement Recommendation

The Department of Justice's approach to combating the theft of intellectual property is most visible in its enforcement of criminal laws, because the Justice Department is aggressively investigating and prosecuting intellectual property crimes. Success in the fight against intellectual property theft, however, also requires aggressive enforcement of civil laws by the owners of intellectual property. Accordingly, the Task Force recommends that the Department of Justice adopt the following recommendation to increase the effectiveness of civil intellectual property enforcement.

Civil Enforcement Recommendation 1#

Support Civil Enforcement of Intellectual Property Laws by Owners of Intellectual Property Rights

Recommendation: The Department of Justice should assist private parties in enforcing civil laws that protect intellectual property owners against theft by supporting an effective statutory framework for such enforcement. When a court decision or lawsuit threatens the civil remedies available under federal law, the Justice Department should defend in court all appropriate intellectual property protections and vigorously defend Congress's authority in protecting intellectual property rights.

Background: The owners of intellectual property often use civil lawsuits effectively to protect their intellectual property rights. In recent years, private owners have obtained numerous judgments and settlements against those who steal their intellectual property. Civil lawsuits have proven to be an effective enforcement method in many types of intellectual property cases.

Over the last several years, one of the greatest emerging threats to intellectual property ownership has been the use of peer-to-peer ("P2P") networks. P2P networks are freely accessible on the Internet and allow users to access and copy data files directly from each others' computers. The use of these networks is widespread, and digital copies of audio and video recordings are the most transferred items. It is estimated that millions of users access P2P networks and that the vast majority of users illegally distribute copyrighted material through the networks. In most instances, these violators are difficult to prosecute criminally for a variety of reasons, including the general lack of a profit motive and the relatively low dollar value often involved. Enforcement is thus generally left to owners of the intellectual property to locate offenders and file civil lawsuits against them.

Private civil enforcement, however, is not always effective. Although illegal P2P file sharing is rampant, the Internet has made tracking illegal file sharing very difficult. For example, users of the Internet must gain access through an Internet Service Provider that assigns an "Internet Protocol Address" to the user. The Internet Protocol Address is a unique number that can be later used to identify the person who used the address. The Internet Service Provider, however, is the sole holder of the information that links the Internet Protocol Address with the identity of the user. Consequently, owners of intellectual property cannot identify users of file sharing programs without the information from the Internet Service Providers.

For years, one of the few legal options available to an owner of a copyright who believed an unknown file sharing user was illegally transmitting copyrighted material was to file a "John Doe" lawsuit against the violator. "John Doe" lawsuits allow the copyright owner, or industry association, to file a lawsuit and start the legal process without knowing the name of the violator. Because Internet Service Providers are not required to maintain records for any length of time, plaintiffs in "John Doe" lawsuits are not always able to obtain a court order in time to identify the violator.

In 1998, Congress provided an alternative to the "John Doe" lawsuits when it enacted the Digital Millennium Copyright Act ("DMCA"). The DMCA allows copyright owners to compel Internet Service Providers to identify alleged infringers by serving a subpoena without having to first file a lawsuit. This legal tool is an improvement in the civil enforcement scheme because it enables copyright owners to move quickly in identifying the name of a suspected violator before any relevant records are erased. Armed with a subpoena, copyright owners can determine who is unlawfully downloading their copyrighted material using P2P networks and then work to resolve the dispute by taking legal action.

Some Internet Service Providers have resisted DMCA subpoenas by contending that the subpoena provision does not apply to their service because they do not store the copyrighted material, but instead only transmit the data. The Justice Department has filed briefs opposing the Internet Service Providers' challenges to the use of the DMCA to identify suspected violators of intellectual property rights and has also defended the constitutionality of the statute.

Explanation: In civil cases where the constitutionality or viability of important civil enforcement tools are at issue, the Department of Justice should intervene by submitting a written brief to the court hearing the case, to protect the use of civil enforcement methods in accordance with federal law. In addition to defending the validity of the DMCA's subpoena provision, the Justice Department has shown its commitment to intervene in cases when other intellectual property laws have come under constitutional attack. Therefore, the Department of Justice should closely monitor civil enforcement developments in the law that may reduce the effectiveness of the private, civil enforcement scheme. When such court decisions arise, the Justice Department must identify them and take affirmative steps to correct them.

D. Antitrust Enforcement Recommendations

The core mission of the Antitrust Division of the Department of Justice is to promote and protect the competitive process and the American economy through enforcement of antitrust laws. These laws prohibit a variety of practices that restrain trade, such as price-fixing conspiracies, corporate mergers likely to reduce competition, and predatory acts designed to achieve or maintain monopoly power. When these practices involve intellectual property, they can raise complex questions about the proper application of antitrust to intellectual property rights. The Department of Justice recognizes that intellectual property rights can promote competition by creating incentives to innovate and commercialize new ideas that enhance consumer welfare. The Department of Justice is also aware that enforcing the antitrust laws in a way that condemns the beneficial use of intellectual property rights could undermine the incentive to create and disseminate intellectual property. The Task Force therefore recommends that the Department of Justice adopt the following recommendations to help ensure that the antitrust laws are appropriately applied to intellectual property in a way that does not chill the exercise of legitimate intellectual property rights.

Antitrust Enforcement Recommendation #1

Support the Rights of Intellectual Property Owners to Determine Independently Whether to License Their Technology

Recommendation: *The Department of Justice should support the rights of intellectual property owners to decide independently whether to license their technology to others.*

Background: It is well established under United States law that an intellectual property owner's decision not to license its technology to others cannot violate the antitrust laws. Nonetheless, some critics of robust intellectual property rights have suggested that antitrust laws should be used to force owners of intellectual property rights to share "essential" technology with others, even when that would require them to assist their competitors.

Explanation: Owners of intellectual property rights should be free to decide independently whether to license their technology to others, without fear of violating the antitrust laws. This was confirmed by a recent legal ruling that expressed great skepticism about applying the antitrust laws in ways that would force companies to share the source of their competitive advantage with others. Although an intellectual property owner has the right to decide not to license its technology, the owner does not have the right to impose conditions on licensees that would effectively extend an intellectual property right beyond its legal limits. The Department of Justice should continue to oppose efforts in the United States and abroad to promote the notion that an independent decision not to license technology is an antitrust violation.

Antitrust Enforcement Recommendation #2

Encourage Use of the Justice Department's Business Review Procedure

Recommendation: *The Department of Justice should encourage trade associations and other business organizations seeking to establish industry standards for the prevention of intellectual property theft, to use the Justice Department's business review procedure for guidance regarding antitrust enforcement concerns.*

Background: Trade associations and other organizations often take steps to develop and adopt uniform standards that will better enable industry participants to protect their intellectual property rights and discourage theft of their intellectual property. Digital rights management software, anti-theft software, and other content protection schemes could, for example, be the subject of such standard-setting activities. However, the process of negotiating standards can raise antitrust concerns. For example, competitors involved in the standard-setting process may use such negotiations as a forum for price fixing and other forms of collusion.

Explanation: The Department of Justice's business review procedure provides trade associations and other business organizations seeking to establish industry standards a valuable opportunity to receive guidance from the Department of Justice with respect to the scope, interpretation, and application of the antitrust laws to proposed standard-setting activities. Under that procedure, persons concerned about whether a particular proposed standard-setting activity is legal under the antitrust laws may ask the Department of Justice for a statement of its current enforcement intentions with respect to that conduct. When sufficient information and documents are submitted to the Department of Justice, the Department will make its best effort to resolve the business review request within sixty to ninety days. In this way, the Department of Justice can protect competition while at the same time facilitate efficient business arrangements that enable intellectual property owners to protect their rights.

Antitrust Enforcement Recommendation #3

Promote International Cooperation on the Application of Antitrust Laws to Intellectual Property Rights

Recommendation: *The Department of Justice should continue to promote international cooperation and principled agreement between nations on the proper application of antitrust laws to intellectual property rights.*

Background: While antitrust and intellectual property laws are often national in scope, competition occurs on an increasingly global scale. Differing application of antitrust and intellectual property law principles in different countries can create inefficiencies for global business, result in antitrust violations in some countries for the use of intellectual property that is legal in others, and even lead to the loss of intellectual property rights in certain nations. If nations can reduce such discrepancies in applying antitrust law to intellectual property, they can reduce inefficiencies and promote vigorous cross-border competition.

Explanation: The Department of Justice should continue to promote principled agreement among nations on the proper application of antitrust law to intellectual property. It should continue its efforts to engage in multinational meetings, formal conferences, and informal outreach with foreign antitrust agencies. Through these efforts, the Department of Justice can ensure that the United States and its trading partners have the benefit of each other's experience in dealing with issues at the intersection of antitrust and intellectual property law. Through the establishment of intellectual property working groups with the European Union, Japan, and Korea, the Department of Justice has discussed a wide variety of intellectual property topics vital to the efficient functioning of the global marketplace of ideas. These working groups foster candid communications between the Department of Justice and foreign antitrust enforcers. The Department of Justice should continue these efforts and expand them to include more United States trading partners, and should also closely monitor developments concerning the application of antitrust to intellectual property...

How Can the Department of Justice Prevent Intellectual Property Crime?

While prosecuting intellectual property crime forms the crux of the Department of Justice's strategy, the Task Force also recognizes that preventing crimes from occurring in the first place is a critical component to any crime-fighting program. Publicizing successful prosecutions is an important way to deter future crimes. In addition, educational initiatives that make clear the consequences of choices made must play a key role in any solution to such a pervasive and complex problem.

Prevention Recommendation #1

Develop a National Education Program to Prevent Intellectual Property Crime

Recommendation: *The Department of Justice should develop a national program to educate students about the value of intellectual property and the consequences of committing intellectual property crimes by: A) Developing materials for student educational programs, B) Creating partnerships with non-profit educational organizations to promote public awareness regarding intellectual property crime, C) Developing a video to teach students about the negative consequences of intellectual property theft, and D) Encouraging federal prosecutors handling intellectual property crime cases throughout the nation to promote the Department of Justice's public awareness programs.*

Background: Prosecuting criminals, civil enforcement, and international cooperation are only some of the methods that can be used to address the problem of intellectual property theft. As in other areas of the law, public awareness and prevention is a necessary dimension in addressing the growing problem of intellectual property theft. Educating the public, and especially the youth of the nation, about intellectual property rights and responsibilities can be an effective method of deterring crime before it happens. In addition, such educational efforts can generate a better understanding of the value of creative works in the nation's economy and the need to protect these valuable economic resources.

Explanation: The Task Force recommends that the Department of Justice develop a national education campaign on intellectual property. This effort would be aimed at teaching students about the value of creativity and innovation, and would send a clear message that intellectual property theft is both illegal and sometimes dangerous. The education campaign, which will be set in motion by the Task Force's launch event, will be expanded nationwide through the United States Attorney's Offices and through interagency partnerships, as well as cooperation with both non-profit organizations and industry.

The Task Force has developed a proposal to launch the national education campaign with a full-day conference for high school students in October 2004. The Justice Department is currently organizing the event. In partnership with CourtTV,[2] and with the help and support of Street Law[3] and i-Safe,[4] the Task Force will bring together about 100 students from high schools in the District of Columbia, Virginia, and Maryland along with teachers, legal experts, and artists, to learn about and discuss intellectual property issues. The conference will feature discussions with diverse speakers representing government, industry, and entertainment; creative presentations by popular artists; workshops aimed at educating the students on the alternatives to illegal downloading and other violations of intellectual property rights; and an opportunity for the students to share their own views and ask questions of the Attorney General and Task Force members.

Such an event can serve as a model for similar conferences nationwide, and may be recorded by CourtTV to produce television programming on intellectual property issues. An authorized recording of the program can be distributed throughout the country for use in public awareness events.

The Task Force also recommends that the Department of Justice work with non-profit organizations to help develop a set of classroom materials regarding intellectual property. By developing partnerships with organizations that promote youth education on intellectual property, the Department of Justice can build upon existing materials and expand educational opportunities throughout the United States.

The Task Force recommends a new private/public education initiative aimed at teaching fifth and sixth graders about the dangers of intellectual property theft. Working in concert with private industry representatives, the Justice Department's Offices of Public Affairs and Intergovernmental and Public Liaison should develop an educational video to teach students about the value of intellectual property and the dangers and consequences of online theft. The initiative should also foster in students an appreciation for genuine and legal works of creativity. This group should explore launching an initiative in the 2005-2006 school year.

Finally, the Task Force recommends that the Department of Justice use the existing network of talented federal prosecutors to promote the Justice Department's public awareness program. Because federal prosecutors are located in particular regions of the country, they can identify crime problems within their region and tailor public awareness efforts to address those problems. Accordingly, the Department of Justice should encourage every CHIP Coordinator to initiate local educational campaigns on intellectual property, using the materials developed by the Justice Department and its education partners. The program may consist of presentations at local schools, one-day student conferences modeled after the launch event mentioned earlier, or other methods that may appeal to students in the particular region.

Prevention Recommendation #2

Educate the Public Regarding the Department of Justice's Policy on Peer-to-Peer Networks

Recommendation: *The Department of Justice should educate the public regarding its policy prohibiting the use of peer-to-peer file sharing networks on Justice Department computer systems.*

Background: The Department of Justice has recognized that peer-to-peer networks may pose a danger to computer systems and are often used to distribute copyrighted materials without authorization. On September 17, 2004, the Chief Information Officer for the Justice Department issued a memorandum to every employee discussing the Department of Justice's policy prohibiting the use of peer-to-peer software on its computer systems. A copy of the memorandum is included in the appendix.

Explanation: The Department of Justice should educate the public about its analysis of peer-to-peer software as a vehicle for distributing unauthorized copies of copyrighted software and the negative effects it can have on computer networks.

Prevention Recommendation #3

Promote Authorized Use and Awareness of The FBI's New Anti-Piracy Seal and Warning.

Recommendation: *The Department of Justice should promote authorized use and awareness of the FBI's new Anti-Piracy Seal to deter copyright infringement and trademark offenses.*

Background: The FBI is expanding the use of its warning message and seal to address intellectual property rights violations. Last year, the FBI together with the Justice Department collaborated to develop a new FBI Seal for intellectual property enforcement purposes. On November 17, 2003, the Attorney General approved the "Anti-Piracy Seal and Warning." The purpose of the new seal is to warn the public that unauthorized duplication of copyrighted works is a federal crime. The FBI has entered into agreements with record and movie associations to include the seal on copyrighted works as part of a pilot program, and is developing additional agreements with the software and video game industry. The program will serve as a model for future widespread application of the seal.

Explanation: The Department of Justice should promote awareness of the FBI's Anti-Piracy Seal and support its continued use on copyrighted works. The Department of Justice should encourage industry associations to use the seal, in accordance with written agreements with the FBI, on copyrighted works to serve as a visible warning of the consequences of committing intellectual property crimes.

Conclusion

This report is not an ending, but a beginning. Under the leadership of the Attorney General, the Task Force looks forward to implementing these recommendations and continuing to improve the performance of the Department of Justice to protect intellectual property.

While technology is constantly advancing, so must the tools and techniques of law enforcement to prevent theft. And as the nation's economy becomes increasingly dependent on intellectual property, law enforcement must work harder to protect that which makes America prosperous.

Notes

1.   The full report is available at http://www.usdoj.gov/olp/ip_task_force_report. pdf
2.   CourtTV is a cable network that specializes in investigative and forensics programming.
3.   Street Law is a non-profit education provider based in Washington, DC. It develops programs and written materials to promote awareness of legal rights and responsibilities and to engage youth and adults in the democratic process.
4.   i-Safe America, Inc., is a non-profit foundation dedicated to ensuring the safe and responsible use of the Internet by the nation's youth. It offers a series of interactive classroom lessons (for all grades, K-12) A curriculum section on intellectual property is first offered in fifth grade, and continues through the twelfth grade.

About the Contributors

Jay S. Albanese is Professor of Government & Public Policy at Virginia Commonwealth University. He served as Chief of the International Center at the National Institute of Justice from 2002-2006. Jay received the Ph.D. and M.A. degrees from Rutgers University and B.A. from Niagara University. Dr. Albanese is author of seven books that include *Criminal Justice* (3rd ed., Allyn & Bacon, 2005), *Organized Crime in Our Times* (4th ed., Lexis/Nexis/Anderson, 2004), *Professional Ethics in Criminal Justice* (Allyn & Bacon, 2006), contributor to *Comparative Criminal Justice Systems* (3rd ed., Wadsworth, 2006), and editor of *Transnational Crime* (de Sitter, 2005). He has written articles on the subjects of human trafficking, obscenity, white-collar and organized crime. Dr. Albanese is Executive Director of the International Association for the Study of Organized Crime (www.iasoc.net). He is a past president of the Academy of Criminal Justice Sciences (ACJS).

Annette Beresford earned her doctorate in 2002, and has published articles on financial crime and anti-terrorism in *Administration & Society* and *The Journal of Homeland Security and Emergency Management*. Dr. Beresford has worked for ten years in government regulation and law enforcement, and served as visiting professor at Florida Atlantic University in 2002-2003 and Research Associate at NW3C in 2003-2004. Currently, Dr. Beresford works in Washington DC with DISB's Enforcement and Investigation Bureau and is a member of the USSS Washington Metro Electronic Crimes Task Force.

Christian Desilets is a graduate of the Georgetown Law Center, where he specialized in Internet, computer, intellectual property, and white-collar crime issues. Before Georgetown, he pursued his academic studies at Mississippi State University, graduating with a degree in sociology, a minor in computer science, and certification in criminal justice and corrections. He was awarded Alpha Kappa Delta's Sociology Undergraduate of the Year award in 1997. Between completing law school and accepting employment at the NW3C, he spent a few months at a patent-oriented legal practice in northern Virginia, primarily researching software and web-based utility patents. His duties as a research attorney include creating and maintaining computerized knowledge-management tools, performing legal research and analysis, and drafting articles of interest to the NW3C community.

Sandy Haantz earned a Bachelor of Art degree in Criminal Justice from Columbia College in Missouri. She began her career as a Securities Investigator with the Securities Division of the Missouri Secretary of State. Her duties included enforcement of state securities regulations and investigation of fraudulent activity involving securities and investments. She joined the NW3C in 1995 where she coordinated development, logistics, and delivery of training. Concurrently, she supported the establishment of the Training and Research Institute that included the training, research, computer crime, and operation sections. Sandy is a Research Assistant in the Research Section where she conducts a broad range of applied research tasks related to economic crime, including project design, data collection, analysis, and report writing.

John Kane is currently Research Manager at the National White Collar Crime Center (NW3C). Prior to joining the NW3C, Kane was a graduate research associate with the Security Research Project, a private grant project at the University of Florida, where he studied various elements of workplace-related crime and deviance. His current areas of interest include identity theft, embezzlement, and Internet-facilitated crime. Kane received both his undergraduate and graduate degrees in Sociology from the University of Florida.

Jeffrey Scott McIllwain is an Associate Professor of Public Administration and Criminal Justice and Associate Director of the Interdisciplinary Graduate Program in Homeland Security at San Diego State University. His organized crime articles have appeared in *Justice Quarterly, Crime, Law & Social Change, Western Legal History*, and *Transnational Organized Crime*, and his first book, *Organizing Crime in Chinatown* (McFarland), was published in 2004.

Hedieh Nasheri is a Professor of Justice Studies at Kent State University and a visiting fellow at the University of London's Institute of Advanced Legal Studies in the U.K. She received her graduate training in social policy and Law (Ph.D. 1992) from Case Western Reserve University. She is author of several books including *Economic Espionage and Industrial Spying* (Cambridge University Press 2005) and numerous journal articles and book reviews. She has written and lectured extensively in the areas of law and social sciences and has given a number of invited lectures nationally and internationally on a wide range of policy and law related topics. Professor Nasheri's research interests pertain to four related topics: Law & Technology, Intellectual Property, Protection of Trade Secrets & Economic Espionage, Cybercrime, and Comparative Jurisprudence.

Nicole Leeper Piquero is an Assistant Professor in the Department of Criminology, Law and Society at the University of Florida. Her current research focuses on the etiology of white-collar crime, personality dimensions and traits associated with white-collar and corporate crime decision-making, and white-collar crime victimization. Her work has appeared in *Justice Quarterly*, *Law and Society Review*, *Journal of Criminal Justice*, and *Youth and Society*.

April Wall is a Research Assistant with the National White Collar Crime Center (NW3C) and a masters student in the Department of Criminology and Criminal Justice at the University of Maryland. Prior to working at NW3C, she worked as a graduate research assistant at the University of Maryland, assisting Dr. Doris MacKenzie with the "What Works in Corrections" initiative. She holds a Bachelor of Arts in Psychology from Concord University and is currently serving as an adjunct faculty member at Fairmont State University where she specializes in the Internet and criminal activity.

Index